INTRODUCING THE NEW TESTAMENT

Zondervan Books by D. A. Carson

Becoming Conversant with the Emerging Church

The Gagging of God

An Introduction to the New Testament
(coauthor with Douglas Moo)

Matthew in the Expositor's Bible Commentary

Telling the Truth (general editor)

Worship by the Book (editor)

Zondervan Books by Douglas J. Moo

2 Peter, Jude in the NIV Application Commentary series

Romans in the NIV Application Commentary series

"Romans," "James," "2 Peter," "Jude" in the
Zondervan *Illustrated Bible Backgrounds Commentary*

An Introduction to the New Testament
(coauthor with D. A. Carson)

a **short guide** to its history and message

INTRODUCING THE NEW TESTAMENT

d.a.
CARSON

douglas j.
MOO

edited by
andrew david
NASELLI

ZONDERVAN®

ZONDERVAN

Introducing the New Testament
An abridgment of *An Introduction to the New Testament*
Copyright © 1992, 2005, 2010 by D. A. Carson and Douglas J. Moo

Requests for information should be addressed to:

Zondervan, 3900 *Sparks Drive SE, Grand Rapids, Michigan* 49546

Library of Congress Cataloging-in-Publication Data
   Carson, D. A.
      Introducing the New Testament : a short guide to its history and message /
   D. A. Carson and Douglas J. Moo ; edited by Andrew David Naselli. — [Abridged
   ed.].
         p. cm.
      Rev. ed. of: An introduction to the New Testament. c2005.
      Includes bibliographical references.
      ISBN 978-0-310-29149-7 (softcover)
      1. Bible. N.T. — Introductions. I. Moo, Douglas J. II. Naselli, Andrew David. III.
   Carson, D. A. Introduction to the New Testament. IV. Title.
   BS2330.3.C37 2010
   225.6'1 — dc22   2009046403

Interior design: Matthew VanZomeren

Printed in the United States of America

CONTENTS

PREFACE

Dear Reader,

You are probably using this book because you are convinced that the Bible is God's Word—and, just for that reason, you are keen to understand it better. But, of course, God has chosen to reveal his Word to us in human words—words written by particular people, in particular situations, to particular people, and about particular problems and issues. Knowing about these particulars helps us to understand just what God in his Word is seeking to tell us. In this book, we outline the circumstances in which God's New Testament Word was written in order to help you understand, appreciate, and live out that Word.

Few of you will read this book at one time from cover to cover. It is a reference book, one that you will want to consult as you read or teach portions of the New Testament. Each book (or, in some cases, a group of books) of the New Testament is profiled in its own chapter. These chapters provide a quick and readable overview of the circumstances in which the book was written, along with an outline of its contents. Other chapters address general topics that arise from a group of New Testament books—the Synoptic Gospels, the letters of the New Testament, the Apostle Paul. We especially encourage you to read, before turning to particular sections in the book, the opening chapter on "Thinking about the Study of the New Testament." This chapter will provide an important orientation for what we say in the rest of the book.

This volume is a condensation of a longer and more detailed treatment of these same issues: *An Introduction to the New Testament* (D. A. Carson and Douglas J. Moo [2d ed.; Grand Rapids: Zondervan, 2005]). We encourage you to consult this longer treatment if you want to go more deeply into any of the issues we cover in this volume. Nevertheless, we are very grateful for the opportunity to put this larger work into a form that can be used by a wider audience. Andy Naselli did a remarkable job of providing an initial draft of this condensation, and we (Don and Doug) are very grateful for his careful work. All three of us hope and pray that as you learn more about the New Testament, you will come to know better and love more dearly the One whom the New Testament speaks of on its every page.

To God be the glory.

—D. A. Carson
Douglas J. Moo
Andrew David Naselli

ABBREVIATIONS

BST	Bible Speaks Today
EBC	The Expositor's Bible Commentary
IVPNTC	InterVarsity Press New Testament Commentary
NAC	New American Commentary
NIBC	New International Bible Commentary
NICNT	New International Commentary on the New Testament
NIV	New International Version of the Bible
NIVAC	New International Version Application Commentary
NRSV	New Revised Standard Version of the Bible
PNTC	Pillar New Testament Commentary
RSV	Revised Standard Version of the Bible
THNTC	Two Horizons New Testament Commentary
TNTC	Tyndale New Testament Commentary

chapter one

THINKING ABOUT THE STUDY OF THE NEW TESTAMENT

People have been reading and studying the New Testament (NT) for as long as its documents have been in existence. Even before all twenty-seven NT books were written, some found the interpretation of the available documents more than a little challenging (see 2 Pet. 3:15–16 on Paul). A distance of two millennia and changes of language, culture, and history have not made the task any less difficult. Furthermore, the overabundance of writings on the NT across the centuries makes the task both easier and harder. It is easier because there are many good guides, and it is harder because the sheer volume and thoroughly mixed nature of the material are profoundly daunting.

About This Book

This book aims to serve you as an introductory guide to understanding the NT. Its layout is straightforward, following the order of the NT books as they occur in our English Bibles. Chapters 2, 8, and 9 introduce groups of NT books, and the rest of the chapters discuss individual NT books, typically answering the following questions (though not always in this order):

1. Content: What is the book about?
2. Author: Who wrote the book?
3. Genre: What style of literature is used?
4. Date: When was the book written?
5. Place: Where was the book written?

6. Audience: To whom was the book written?
7. Purpose: Why was the book written?
8. Contributions: What does the book contribute to our understanding of the faith?

Most of the space in the chapters is dedicated to content and contributions. We suggest that you read this book with an open Bible, perhaps reading each NT book in its entirety as you work through the opening section on its content. The many headings and numbered lists make the material user-friendly with easy-to-find summaries of key points.

Each chapter ends by asking some questions for review and discussion and listing recommended resources for further reading. Below are some general resources that may aid you as you advance in your study of the NT.

Recommended Resources

Introductory

Blomberg, Craig L. *Jesus and the Gospels: An Introduction and Survey.* 2d ed. Nashville: Broadman & Holman, 2009.

———. *From Pentecost to Patmos: An Introduction to Acts through Revelation.* Nashville: Broadman & Holman, 2006.

Burge, Gary M., Lynn H. Cohick, and Gene L. Green. *The New Testament in Antiquity: A Survey of the New Testament within Its Cultural Contexts.* Grand Rapids: Zondervan, 2009.

Carson, D. A. "Approaching the Bible." Pages 1–19 in *New Bible Commentary: 21st Century Edition.* Edited by D. A. Carson, R. T. France, J. A. Motyer, and G. J. Wenham. 4th ed. Downers Grove: InterVarsity Press, 1994. (This article gives a basic overview to interpreting the Bible.)

Elwell, Walter A., and Robert W. Yarbrough, eds. *Encountering the New Testament: A Historical and Theological Survey.* 2d ed. Grand Rapids: Baker, 2005. (This book gives a trustworthy, readable overview with dozens of color pictures and an interactive CD-ROM.)

The ESV Study Bible. Wheaton: Crossway Bibles, 2008. (This Bible contains useful articles and concise introductions and notes for each book.)

TNIV Study Bible. Grand Rapids: Zondervan, 2006. (This Bible contains concise introductions and notes for each book.)

Intermediate

Alexander, T. Desmond, and Brian S. Rosner, eds. *New Dictionary of Biblical Theology*. Downers Grove: InterVarsity Press, 2000. (This book has three parts: [1] twelve major introductory articles, e.g., D. A. Carson, "Systematic Theology and Biblical Theology," pp. 89–104; [2] seven articles on the most important collections of biblical writings followed by articles on each book of the Bible; and [3] 140 articles on major biblical themes.)

Evans, Craig A., and Stanley E. Porter, eds. *Dictionary of New Testament Background*. Downers Grove: InterVarsity Press, 2000.

Green, Joel B., and Scot McKnight, eds. *Dictionary of Jesus and the Gospels*. Downers Grove: InterVarsity Press, 1992.

Hawthorne, Gerald F., and Ralph P. Martin, eds. *Dictionary of Paul and His Letters*. Downers Grove: InterVarsity Press, 1993.

Keener, Craig S. *The IVP Bible Background Commentary: New Testament*. Downers Grove: InterVarsity Press, 1993.

Martin, Ralph P., and Peter H. Davids, eds. *Dictionary of the Later New Testament and Its Developments*. Downers Grove: InterVarsity Press, 1997. (See especially D. A. Carson, "New Testament Theology," pp. 796–814.)

Advanced

Black, David Alan, and David S. Dockery, eds. *Interpreting the New Testament: Essays on Methods and Issues*. Nashville: Broadman & Holman, 2001.

Carson, D. A. *New Testament Commentary Survey*. 6th ed. Grand Rapids: Baker, 2007. (Carson briefly evaluates hundreds of NT commentaries.)

Thielman, Frank. *Theology of the New Testament: A Canonical and Synthetic Approach*. Grand Rapids: Zondervan, 2005. (This book is user-friendly for students, cautious, gentle, understated, and edifying.)

chapter two

THE SYNOPTIC GOSPELS

A. What Are the Synoptic Gospels?

The first three gospels—Matthew, Mark, and Luke—are often called the Synoptic Gospels. "Synoptic" means "seeing together," and the description is appropriate since Matthew, Mark, and Luke (in contrast to John) are highly similar in three ways:

1. Structure: They structure Jesus' ministry according to a general geographic sequence: Galilee, withdrawal to the north, Judea and Perea, and Jerusalem. In contrast, John focuses on Jesus' ministry in Jerusalem during his periodic visits to the city.
2. Content: They recount many of the same events, focusing on Jesus' healings, exorcisms, and teachings in parables. In contrast, John does not recount exorcisms, parables of the kind we find in the Synoptics, or many other events (e.g., the sending out of the Twelve, the transfiguration, the Olivet Discourse, the Last Supper).
3. Tone: They convey a tone of intense, rapid-fire action with Jesus' constant travels, actions (especially miracles), and (usually) brief teachings. In contrast, John's tone is more meditative, recounting fewer events and longer discourses.

Over the last two centuries, scholars have scrutinized the Synoptic Gospels from many angles and with many different results. This is inevitable, given the vital importance of these books for Christian belief and life. These books narrate the life of Jesus, the One whom God has chosen especially to make himself known to human beings.

They depict the events on which the significance of history and the destiny of every single individual depend: the death and resurrection of Jesus the Messiah.

B. How Did the Synoptic Gospels Come into Being?

Simply identifying the authors of the Synoptic Gospels leaves some questions unanswered. How did the authors get the material about Jesus that they used? Why are the three accounts so similar at so many places and so different at others? Were the evangelists themselves recorders of tradition or authors with their own point of view? And to raise the larger question that lurks behind all of these, why *four* gospels?

Luke refers to three stages in which the gospel material has come to him (Luke 1:1–4):

1. Oral traditions: "Eyewitnesses and servants of the word" "handed down" the truth about Jesus.
2. Written sources: "Many" have already drawn up accounts of Jesus and the early church.
3. Final composition: Luke himself, having "carefully investigated" these sources, now composes his own "orderly" account.

In studies of the gospels over the last two centuries, scholars have developed distinct methods focusing on each of these stages. The three sections below are simple sketches of complex issues with which Bible interpreters continue to wrestle.

Each of these approaches may be either fruitful or harmful depending on how one uses them. Many scholars have employed them in harmful ways and reached damning conclusions. For example, some reject that the gospels recount real history and thus deny the historicity of Jesus' resurrection.

The Stage of Oral Traditions: Form Criticism

Form criticism assesses the stage when the early Christians passed on the words and actions of Jesus by word of mouth. Form critics claim that only after two decades or so did the material begin to be put into written sources, with the gospels themselves coming shortly afterward. During this time, the various stories about Jesus were molded into distinct "forms" by the early Christians. The attempt to isolate these forms can be useful, but many form critics have made the mistake of thinking that the early church significantly changed the oral tradition as it was passed on. There is no good reason for such a negative historical judgment.

The Stage of Written Sources: Source Criticism (the Synoptic Problem)

As time moved on, early written fragments were combined with oral testimony to produce lengthier written sources and, finally, the gospels. Source criticism seeks to identify the written sources used to make up the three Synoptic Gospels. They are strikingly similar in both general outline and particular wording (e.g., cf. Matt. 9:1–8; Mark 2:1–12; Luke 5:17–26). They also have puzzling differences.

The "synoptic problem" is the predicament of coming up with a comprehensive explanation of both the similarities and differences in the Synoptic Gospels. This, then, is the question behind the synoptic problem: What theory best accounts for the combination of exact agreement and wide divergence that characterizes the first three gospels?

There are two main options:

1. Matthew, Mark, and Luke were written independently of one another, but they are similar because they depend on a common source (or sources): an original gospel, oral sources, or developing written fragments.
2. Matthew, Mark, and Luke depend on each other. Two of the evangelists used one or more of the other gospels in constructing their own. This solution to the synoptic problem has been urged from early on in the history of the church, and it commands almost universal assent among contemporary NT scholars — with good reason. This theory of interdependence provides the best explanation of how God has chosen to bring our first three gospels into existence.

There are currently two main versions of the interdependence theory. (1) The "two-gospel" solution proposes that Luke used Matthew to write his gospel and then Mark used both Matthew and Luke. (2) A more convincing explanation of the data, properly nuanced, is the "two-source" theory. Matthew and Luke independently used two sources: Mark and "Q," a lost collection of Jesus' sayings (Q abbreviates the German word *Quelle*, which means "source"). This means that Mark was written first. Then Matthew and Luke borrowed from

Mark and Q, but not from each other. A source like Q remains the best explanation for the agreements between Matthew and Luke in non-Markan material. There are two caveats, however, to the two-source theory:

1. The process through which the gospels came into being was so complex that *no* theory, however detailed, can hope to provide a complete explanation.
2. This theory cannot satisfactorily explain some data, so we should treat it more as a working theory than as a fixed conclusion.

The Stage of Final Composition: Redaction Criticism

Redaction criticism assesses the theological purposes of the evangelists by analyzing the way they used their sources. "Redaction" refers to the process of editing oral and written traditions as a gospel was actually written. Critiquing this editorial activity involves examining what the authors include and exclude and how they arrange, connect, and word the material. Patterns may indicate theological concerns (e.g., Luke emphasizes prayer). Hardly any serious study of the Gospels proceeds without use of some kind of redaction criticism. It becomes problematic when it makes exaggerated claims, false assumptions, and inappropriate applications. Pursued properly, however, redaction criticism has positive benefits:

1. It is more helpful than form and source criticism because it focuses on the final text of the gospels.
2. It reminds us that the evangelists wrote with more than—but not less than—historical interest. Rearranging, adding, omitting, and rewording need not detract from the historicity of the event or teaching concerned. For instance, newspapers will frequently rewrite for their own readers news-service reports that they receive, but their rewrites need not affect the accuracy of the report. Major speeches will sometimes be summarized in a few words, or excerpts will be taken from them. In doing so, different newspapers may focus on different emphases in the same speech. We do not accuse these newspapers of inaccuracy in doing this, nor should we accuse the evangelists of historical inaccuracies if they summarize, excerpt, or reword Jesus' own sayings.
3. It recognizes—and increases our appreciation of—the rich diversity of the gospels. The story of Jesus has come to us not in one super-gospel, but in four gospels, each with its own distinct

and important contribution to make to our understanding of Jesus.

C. What Style of Literature Are the Gospels?

Nowhere in the NT is any of the four accounts of Jesus' ministry called a gospel. The NT uses "gospel" and the related verb "preach the gospel" to denote the message of God's saving act in his Son (e.g., in Mark 1:14–15; Rom. 1:16; 1 Cor. 15:1; Gal. 1:6–7). The early church added the title "gospel" to Matthew, Mark, Luke, and John. These four titles preserve the stress on the singleness of *the* gospel by the way they are phrased: not "the gospel *by* Matthew," but "the [one] gospel, according to [the version of] Matthew" (and Mark, Luke, and John). No books before our gospels had ever been given this designation.

So what style of literature (that is, genre) are the gospels? Accurate interpretation depends to some extent on accurate decisions about the style of literature. Jesus' walking on the water will mean one thing for those who take the gospels to be straightforward history and a very different thing for those who treat them as myth.

The most popular and defensible suggestion is that the gospels are biographies. True, they are quite different from the standard modern biography: they lack accounts of Jesus' childhood development and education, his character and motivations, and chronological precision. But ancient Greco-Roman biographies did not always contain such features either.

The gospels do, however, have features not shared with most other ancient biographies. For example, the authors do not identify themselves by name, and the gospels uniquely combine teaching and action in preaching-oriented writings.

D. What Do the Gospels Tell Us about the Historical Outline of Jesus' Life?

Attempting to construct a historical outline of Jesus' life is important because the truth of what the evangelists are saying is inevitably tied to real history. However, doing so raises a few questions:

1. Is it possible to construct a historical outline of Jesus' life? Yes and no. It is possible to construct a general outline, but it is not possible to construct a detailed, fully satisfactory one. The gos-

pels exhibit a high degree of coherence about the general course of Jesus' ministry as well as about many of the incidents within that ministry. But they simply do not provide us with the kind of chronological and geographic detail that we would need to construct a detailed "life of Jesus." The evangelists narrate historical facts, but they so select, arrange, and present these facts that little information of the kind needed to piece together a detailed life of Jesus is available. They often arrange events topically rather than chronologically.

2. Is this inability to construct a detailed historical outline problematic? No, it was simply not the evangelists' intention to provide us with the kind of data necessary for that. This means that while there is nothing wrong with attempts at harmonizing the accounts (that is, explaining how different accounts of the same event can be fit together historically), we will often have to admit that we just do not know how to fit all the data together. We can continue to assume that if we knew enough, all the data would "fit."

3. How precisely can we date key events in Jesus' life? Setting the events of the gospels against the background of secular history is made easy by the references to well-known historical people, such as Herod the Great (Matthew 2), Caesar Augustus (Luke 2:1), Herod Antipas (Luke 23:6–12), and Pontius Pilate (Matthew 27). The secular timelines have helped us establish these dates in Jesus' life:
   a. Jesus' birth: 6–4 B.C.
   b. The beginning of Jesus' ministry: probably A.D. 28 or 29 (possibly A.D. 25 or 26, or 26 or 27)
   c. The length of Jesus' ministry: at least two years
   d. The death of Jesus: probably Friday, Nisan (a Jewish month that overlaps with our March-April) 14 or 15, A.D. 30 (possibly Friday, Nisan 14, A.D. 33)

E. Questions for Review and Discussion

1. Why are Matthew, Mark, and Luke called the "Synoptic Gospels"?
2. What is the "synoptic problem"?
3. How do the gospels differ from modern biographies?
4. Is the inability to construct a detailed historical outline of Jesus' life problematic? Explain your answer.

F. Recommended Resources

Introductory

Blomberg, Craig L. *Jesus and the Gospels: An Introduction and Survey*. 2d ed. Nashville: Broadman & Holman, 2009.

Boyd, Gregory A., and Paul R. Eddy. *Lord or Legend? Wrestling with the Jesus Dilemma*. Grand Rapids: Baker, 2007.

Roberts, Mark D. *Can We Trust the Gospels? Investigating the Reliability of Matthew, Mark, Luke, and John*. Wheaton: Crossway, 2007.

Intermediate

Blomberg, Craig L. *The Historical Reliability of the Gospels*. 2d ed. Downers Grove: InterVarsity Press, 2007.

Bock, Darrell L. *Jesus according to Scripture: Restoring the Portrait from the Gospels*. Grand Rapids: Baker, 2002.

Stein, Robert H. *Studying the Synoptic Gospels: Origin and Interpretation*. 2d ed. Grand Rapids: Baker, 2001.

Strauss, Mark L. *Four Portraits, One Jesus: An Introduction to Jesus and the Gospels*. Grand Rapids: Zondervan, 2007.

Advanced

Barnett, Paul. *Jesus and the Rise of Early Christianity: A History of New Testament Times*. Downers Grove: InterVarsity Press, 1999.

Black, David Alan, and David R. Beck, eds. *Rethinking the Synoptic Problem*. Grand Rapids: Baker, 2001.

Carson, D. A. "Redaction Criticism: On the Legitimacy and Illegitimacy of a Literary Tool." Pages 119–42, 376–81 in *Scripture and Truth*. Edited by D. A. Carson and John D. Woodbridge. Grand Rapids: Zondervan, 1983.

France, R. T. "The Authenticity of the Sayings of Jesus." Pages 101–41 in *History, Criticism, and Faith*. Edited by Colin Brown. Downers Grove: InterVarsity Press, 1976.

chapter three

MATTHEW

A. What Is Matthew About?

Matthew was a skilled literary craftsman. He presents five discourses, each of which begins in a specific context and ends with a
formula found nowhere else: literally, "And it happened, when Jesus
had finished saying these things, that ..." (7:28–29; 11:1; 13:53;
19:1; 26:1). Five times Matthew alternates between narrative (stories
about Jesus) and discourse (Jesus' teaching).

1. Prologue (1:1–2:23)
    An Old Testament (OT) quotation, introduced by an appro-
    priate fulfillment formula, dominates all but the first of these
    six sections:
    a. Jesus' genealogy (1:1–17)
    b. Jesus' birth (1:18–25)
    c. Visit of the Magi (2:1–12)
    d. Escape to Egypt (2:13–15)
    e. Massacre at Bethlehem (2:16–18)
    f. Return to Nazareth (2:19–23)
2. The gospel of the kingdom (3:1–7:29)
    a. Narrative (3:1–4:25). Matthew recounts John the Bap-
       tist's ministry (3:1–12), Jesus' baptism (3:13–17), Jesus'
       temptation (4:1–11), and Jesus' early Galilean ministry
       (4:12–25).
    b. Discourse of the Sermon on the Mount (5:1–7:29). Jesus
       introduces the kingdom of heaven's norms (5:3–12)
       and witness (5:13–16), explaining its relation to the OT
       (5:17–48). He warns against hypocrisy (6:1–18) in con-
       trast to pursuing kingdom perspectives (6:19–34). The

demand for balance and perfection fulfills OT expectations (7:1–12). People must choose between two ways, two trees, two claims, and two builders (7:13–27). The closing verses reaffirm Jesus' authority (7:28–29).

3. The kingdom extended under Jesus' authority (8:1–11:1)

 a. Narrative (8:1–10:4). This includes a number of miracles, each symbol-laden to portray some facet of the kingdom and its king. It also depicts Matthew's calling (9:9) and Jesus' insistence on eating with public sinners (9:10–13) while announcing that the dawning kingdom, manifest in his own presence, was a time for joy (9:14–17). It ends with the demand for prayer for more workers (9:35–38) and the commissioning of the Twelve (10:1–4).

 b. Discourse on mission and martyrdom (10:5–11:1). After describing the immediate mission (10:5–16), Jesus warns of future sufferings (10:17–25); prohibits fear in the light of the Father's providence (10:26–31); and describes authentic discipleship (10:32–39). Responding to such disciples is equivalent to responding to Jesus himself (10:40–42).

4. Teaching and preaching the gospel of the kingdom: rising opposition (11:2–13:53)

 a. Narrative (11:2–12:50). This not only establishes the relative roles of John the Baptist and of Jesus in the stream of redemptive history (11:2–19); it also reverses public expectations by reporting Jesus' strong condemnation of the "good" Jewish religious towns of Galilee and by announcing relief and rest to the weary and broken—provided they find it in the context of the Son's "yoke" (11:20–30). Tension mounts as Sabbath conflicts erupt (12:1–14), Jesus proves to be more a meek and suffering servant than a visibly conquering king (12:15–21), and confrontation develops not only between Jesus and the Pharisees (12:22–45) but also between Jesus and his own family (12:46–50).

 b. Discourse (13:1–53). The reversal of expectations is a major theme of the kingdom parables.

5. The glory and the shadow: progressive polarization (13:54–19:2)

 a. Narrative (13:54–17:27). This series of vignettes reflects rising polarization (e.g., rejection at Nazareth, 13:54–58; Herod and Jesus, 14:1–12; demands for a sign, 16:1–4) and a profound misunderstanding of the nature and focus of Jesus' power (e.g., the feeding of the five thousand, 14:13–21; see also 14:22–15:20; 17:1–20[21]). The high point is Peter's confession of Jesus (16:13–20), but the aftermath—the first passion prediction (16:21–23; cf. the second in 17:22–23)—shows how little even he has understood.

b. Discourse on life under kingdom authority (18:1–19:2). Greatness is tied to humility (18:3–4); few sins are more odious than causing believers to sin (18:5–9); saving lost sheep is more important than merely nurturing safe sheep (18:10–14); and believers must forgive and practice discipline in the messianic community (18:15–35).

6. Opposition and eschatology: the triumph of grace (19:3–26:5)

a. Narrative (19:3–23:39). Exchanges and parables stress the surprising conduct expected of those who would follow Jesus (19:3–20:34). The events of Passion Week include Jesus' triumphal entry (21:1–11), cleansing the temple (21:12–17), cursing the fig tree (21:18–22), and controversies in the temple court focused on his messianic claims (21:23–22:46). Exasperated, Jesus pronounces his woes on the teachers of the law and the Pharisees (23:1–36) and laments over Jerusalem (23:37–39).

b. The Olivet Discourse (24:1–25:46). Notoriously difficult to interpret, this begins with the setting overlooking the temple (24:1–3). It describes the birth pains of the period between Jesus' two comings (24:4–28); describes the coming of the Son of Man (24:29–31); reflects on the significance of the birth pains (24:32–35); and urges the need to be prepared since the timing of the Son's coming is unknown (24:36–41). A series of parables presents variations on the theme of watchfulness (24:42–25:46). The transitional conclusion includes this gospel's fourth major passion prediction and some details of the plot against Jesus (26:1–5).

7. Jesus' passion and resurrection (26:6–28:20)

a. Passion. The anointing at Bethany (26:6–13) and Judas's betrayal agreement (26:14–16) are rapidly followed by the Last Supper (26:17–30), a prediction of abandonment and denial (26:31–35), Gethsemane (26:36–46), Jesus' arrest (26:47–56), Jesus before the Sanhedrin (26:57–68), Peter's denial of Jesus (26:69–75), the Sanhedrin's formal decision (27:1–2), Judas Iscariot's death (27:3–10), Jesus before Pilate (27:11–26), the soldiers' treatment of Jesus (27:27–31), Jesus' crucifixion and mocking (27:32–44), Jesus' death and its immediate impact (27:45–56), Jesus' burial (27:57–61), and the guard at the tomb (27:62–66).

b. Resurrection. These stories (28:1–17) climax in the Great Commission (28:18–20).

B. Who Wrote Matthew?

Scholars frequently assert that the four gospels are anonymous, that is, the authors do not identify themselves by name. That claim is technically correct if the standard of comparison is, say, Paul's letter to the Romans, where the opening lines clearly state both the author and the initial readers. The gospels according to Matthew, Mark, Luke, and John never explicitly say who wrote them. Nevertheless, we have no evidence that these gospels ever circulated without titles like "according to Matthew." The titles were likely part of the works from the beginning, and the expression "according to" introduces the person understood to be the author. The *one* gospel circulated in four distinct forms: "according to Matthew," "according to Mark," "according to Luke," and "according to John."

The author of Matthew was likely the apostle, "Matthew the tax collector" (10:3). At one level very little hangs on the question of the authorship of this gospel. Neither its meaning nor its authority is greatly changed if one decides that its author was not an apostle.

C. Where Was Matthew Written?

We cannot be certain where Matthew wrote this gospel. Syria is the most likely suggestion, since Antioch of Syria had a large Jewish population and was the first center for Gentile outreach, but nothing of importance hangs on the conclusion.

D. When Was Matthew Written?

Many modern scholars hold that Matthew was written between A.D. 80 and 100, but most of the reasons for this date depend on a network of disputed judgments. The majority of evidence suggests that Matthew was published not long before A.D. 70. For instance, the early church fathers are unanimous in assigning Matthew an early date. Furthermore, some sayings of Jesus might be taken to indicate that the temple, which was destroyed in A.D. 70, was still standing when Matthew wrote (5:23–24; 12:5–7; 23:16–22; cf. 26:60–61).

E. To Whom Was Matthew Written?

The usual assumption is that Matthew wrote this gospel to meet the needs of believers in his own area, which may have had a large Jewish population (e.g., Palestine or Syria). Since the book has so many Jewish features, it is not easy to imagine that the author had a *predominantly* Gentile audience in mind. But it is not implausible to suggest that Matthew wrote his gospel with certain *kinds* of readers in mind, rather than readers in a particular location. There are strong arguments that the Gospels were first written to be read by *all* Christians.

F. Why Was Matthew Written?

Matthew did not directly state his purpose in writing, so all attempts at describing it are inferences drawn from his themes and from the way he treats certain topics as compared with the way the other gospels treat similar topics. Since Matthew's dominant themes are several, complex, and to some extent disputed, it would be difficult to delineate a single narrow purpose.

If we restrict ourselves to widely recognized themes, it is fair to infer that Matthew's purpose is to communicate at least five themes:

1. Jesus is the promised Messiah, the Son of David, the Son of God, the Son of Man, Immanuel, the one to whom the OT points.
2. Many Jews, especially Jewish leaders, sinfully failed to recognize Jesus during his ministry.
3. The promised future kingdom has already dawned, inaugurated by Jesus' life, death, resurrection, and exaltation.
4. This messianic reign is continuing in the world as believers, both Jews and Gentiles, submit to Jesus' authority, overcome temptation, endure persecution, wholeheartedly embrace Jesus' teaching, and thus demonstrate that they are the people of God and the true witness to the world of the "gospel of the kingdom."
5. This messianic reign is not only the fulfillment of OT hopes but the foretaste of the consummated kingdom that will dawn when Jesus the Messiah personally returns.

Matthew designed these complex themes to meet diverse needs, such as catechizing and equipping the church.

G. What Does Matthew Contribute to Our Understanding of the Faith?

Because of the tight relationships among the Synoptic Gospels, the contribution made by any one of them must be evaluated in light of the contribution made by all three. Collectively, the gospels are an irreplaceable, foundational witness to Jesus' person, ministry, teaching, passion, and resurrection. Individually, each provides its own perspective. Matthew has at least six peculiar emphases:

1. Discourses. Matthew preserves large blocks of Jesus' teaching in the five major discourses mentioned above.
2. Virginal conception. Matthew complements Luke by giving an alternative account of Jesus' virginal conception, cast in Joseph's perspective. Quite apart from other stories in the birth narrative of which there is no other record (e.g., the visit of the Magi, the flight into Egypt), the whole account is strongly tied to the OT.
3. Use of the OT. Matthew's use of the OT is particularly rich and complex. The most noticeable peculiarity is the number of OT quotations (estimated between ten and fourteen) found only in Matthew and introduced by a fulfillment formula. Matthew appreciates the links between the old covenant and the new. His notion of prophecy and fulfillment cannot be reduced to mere verbal prediction and historical fulfillment in raw events (though it sometimes includes such a notion). He employs various forms of typology and reads the OT in a Christ-centered way.
4. Law. Many think that Matthew internalizes the law, radicalizes it, subsumes it under the love command, absolutizes only its moral dimensions, or treats it as a schoolmaster that conducts people to Christ. But it is better to use Matthew's own category: Jesus comes to "fulfill" the law (5:17). Thus, the law has a designed, prophetic function.
5. Israel and the church. Matthew is foundational not only as one looks backward to the OT but also as one looks forward to what the church would become. The later debates on the relation between Israel and the church find much of their genesis in Matthew, John, Romans, and Hebrews. Matthew contributes especially to our understanding of Jewish leaders.
6. Jesus. Most of what is central in Matthew's portrayal of Jesus is *not* unique, but it does portray Jesus distinctively. Matthew

may achieve such shading by associating a particular title with some theme, as when he repeatedly links "Son of David" with Jesus' healing ministry. He may also do it by introducing titles of which the other evangelists make no mention, as when he insists that Jesus is Immanuel, "God with us" (1:23).

H. Questions for Review and Discussion

1. What are Matthew's five discourses about?
2. Why is it better to discern multiple purposes for why Matthew wrote this gospel rather than to delineate a single narrow purpose?
3. How does Matthew distinctly portray Jesus?

I. Recommended Resources

Introductory

Carson, D. A. *God with Us: Themes from Matthew.* Brentwood: JKO, 1995. (This book is designed for home Bible studies and adult Sunday school classes.)

————. *Jesus' Sermon on the Mount and His Confrontation with the World: An Exposition of Matthew 5 – 10.* Grand Rapids: Global Christian Publishers, 1999.

Wilkins, Matthew J. *Matthew.* NIVAC. Grand Rapids: Zondervan, 2003.

Intermediate

Blomberg, Craig L. *Matthew.* NAC 22. Nashville: Broadman, 1992.

Carson, D. A. "Matthew." In *Matthew – Luke.* Rev. ed. EBC 9. Grand Rapids: Zondervan, 2010.

Advanced

France, R. T. *The Gospel of Matthew.* NICNT. Grand Rapids: Eerdmans, 2007.

chapter four

MARK

A. What Is Mark About?

Mark's story of Jesus' ministry is action-oriented. Rather than recounting Jesus' extended teaching, Mark shifts scenes rapidly. The book uses the word often translated "immediately" forty-two times (nearly three times as frequently as the rest of the NT). Constantly on the move, Jesus heals, casts out demons, confronts opponents, and instructs the disciples.

1. Preliminaries to the ministry (1:1–13). "The beginning of the good news about Jesus the Messiah" (1:1) consists in the ministry of Jesus' forerunner, John the Baptist (1:2–8), Jesus' baptism by John (1:9–11), and Jesus' temptation by Satan in the wilderness (1:12–13).

2. Galilean ministry, part 1 (1:14–3:6). The summary about Jesus' entrance into Galilee and preaching about God's kingdom is a transition statement in Mark's fast-paced story (1:14–15). After Jesus calls four disciples (1:16–20), Mark gives us a glimpse of a typical day in Jesus' ministry, including teaching in the synagogue, casting out demons, and healings (1:21–34). The extraordinary nature of these events attracts great crowds of people, but Jesus insists on moving to other towns in Galilee (1:35–39). After another healing story (1:40–45), Mark recounts Jesus' disputes with Jewish leaders over his claim to be able to forgive sins (2:1–12), his fellowship with "tax collectors and 'sinners'" (2:13–17), his disciples' failure to fast regularly (2:18–22), and the Sabbath (2:23–3:6).

3. Galilean ministry, part 2 (3:7–5:43). Mark's next transition statement focuses on Jesus' immense popularity and ministry of

healing and casting out demons (3:7–12). This section focuses especially on the kingdom. It begins with Jesus' appointment of twelve "apostles" (3:13–19) and the growing opposition to Jesus on the part of both Jesus' family and "the teachers of the law" (3:20–34). Jesus uses parables to explain this opposition as part of "the secret of the kingdom of God" (4:1–34). The section climaxes with four miracles, each representing a characteristic type of Jesus' miracles: calming the storm (nature, 4:35–41); casting out a "legion" of demons from a man (exorcism, 5:1–20); healing a woman with a flow of blood (healing, 5:25–34); and raising Jairus's daughter from the dead (resurrection, 5:21–24, 35–43).

4. Galilean ministry, part 3 (6:1–8:26). Mark transitions with the story of Jesus' movement away from the region of the Sea of Galilee (where so much of the action of 1:16–5:43 takes place) to his hometown of Nazareth in Galilee's hill country (6:1–6). This section again focuses on Jesus' amazing feats of power, his criticism of certain Jewish customs, and the growing opposition to him. Jesus sends the Twelve out on a mission (6:7–13). The rumor that Jesus is John the Baptist returned from the dead, mentioned along with other popular estimates of his person, leads Mark to include a flashback-explanation of John's death at the hands of Herod Antipas (6:14–29). After the Twelve return, the press of the crowd forces Jesus and his disciples into the wilderness, where he feeds the five thousand (6:30–44). Then Jesus walks on the water as he meets his disciples crossing the Sea of Galilee (6:45–52). He heals many people (6:53–56), explains the real nature of impurity in response to Jewish criticism (7:1–23), and leaves Galilee (and Israel) for the regions of Tyre and Sidon to the North, where he commends the faith of a Gentile woman (7:24–30). Jesus returns to the regions around the Sea of Galilee, healing (7:31–37), feeding the four thousand (8:1–13), teaching the "blinded" disciples (8:14–21), and healing a physically blinded man (8:22–26).

5. The way of glory and suffering (8:27–10:52). Mark transitions with his gospel's climax: Peter recognizes that Jesus is the Messiah (8:27–30). The emphasis shifts from the crowds and Jesus' miraculous power to the disciples and the cross. The heart of this section is a thrice-repeated sequence that embodies a central purpose of Mark at this point in his narrative: Jesus' followers must imitate their Master by humbling themselves and serving others.

a. Jesus predicts his death

8:31	9:30–31	10:32–34

b. The disciples misunderstand

8:32–33	9:32 (33–34)	10:35–40

c. Jesus teaches about the cost of discipleship

8:34–38	9:35–37	10:41–45

Events in this section include Jesus' transfiguration (9:1–13) and a demon being driven out of a young lad (9:14–29). Jesus also teaches here about putting others first (9:38–50), divorce (10:1–12), humility (10:13–16), and the difficulty of combining wealth with discipleship (10:17–31). This section concludes with his giving sight to Bartimaeus in Jericho (10:46–52).

6. Final ministry in Jerusalem (11:1–13:37). This section recounts confrontations between Jesus and various Jewish groups and authorities preceding his passion. Jesus' public entry into Jerusalem sets the stage for the confrontation (11:1–11), and his cleansing the temple forces the issue (11:12–19). The withering of the fig tree is both a lesson in faith and a parable of Israel's judgment (11:20–25). It is thus no surprise that we find "the chief priests, the teachers of the law and the elders" challenging Jesus' authority (11:27–33), or Jesus telling a parable in which the Jewish leaders' rebelliousness to God is a prominent theme (12:1–12). Some Pharisees and Herodians question Jesus about the appropriateness of paying taxes to a Gentile ruler (12:13–17). Sadducees ask about implications of the resurrection (12:18–27), and a teacher of the law asks about the law's greatest commandment (12:28–34). Finally, Jesus takes the initiative, asking about the interpretation of Psalm 110:1 in an effort to force the Jews to consider his claims to be the Messiah (12:35–40). Jesus commends a widow's sacrificial giving (12:41–44), and his Olivet Discourse encourages the disciples to be faithful in light of future suffering as they look toward his triumphant return in glory (13:1–37).

7. The passion and empty-tomb narratives (14:1–16:8). Mark transitions to the story of Jesus' passion with his only mention of a definite date: two days before the Passover, the chief priests and teachers of the law plot Jesus' death (14:1–2). The story of Jesus' anointing in Bethany, which took place "six days before the Pass-

over" (John 12:1–8), is found here for topical reasons: anointing Jesus' head points to his royal dignity (14:3–9). As Judas provides a means of arresting Jesus quietly, Jesus arranges for himself and the disciples to celebrate Passover together (14:10–26). After this meal, during which he uses elements of the Passover ritual to refer to his death, Jesus and the disciples leave the city for Gethsemane on the Mount of Olives where Jesus, after a time of agonizing prayer, is arrested (14:27–52). There follows the series of judicial proceedings and trials: a nighttime hearing before the supreme Jewish council, the Sanhedrin (14:53–65), during which Peter denies the Lord (14:66–72); a quick morning trial before the Sanhedrin (15:1); and the decisive trial before the Roman procurator, Pontius Pilate (15:2–15). Pilate sentences Jesus to death by crucifixion, and the soldiers mock him and execute him at Golgotha (15:16–41). The burial takes place that same day (15:42–47), but the despair of the women who saw him buried gives way to awe at the empty tomb and the angel's announcement of the resurrection (16:1–8).

(See below: "G. Is Mark 16:9–20 Authentic?")

B. Who Wrote Mark?

Mark is anonymous. The title "According to Mark" indicates that by about A.D. 125 an important segment of the early church thought that a person named Mark wrote the second gospel. It is almost certain that "Mark" is the (John) Mark mentioned in Acts (12:12, 25; 13:5, 13; 15:37) and in four NT letters (Col. 4:10; Phlm. 24; 2 Tim. 4:11; 1 Pet. 5:13). No other early Christian Mark would have been so well known as to be mentioned without further description.

Mark's connection with the second gospel is asserted or assumed by many early Christian writers. Papias, bishop of Hierapolis until about A.D. 130, made three important claims (apparently citing the apostle John):

1. Mark wrote the gospel that was identified with this name.
2. Mark was not an eyewitness but obtained his information from Peter.
3. Mark's gospel lacks rhetorical or artistic "order," reflecting the occasional nature of Peter's preaching.

There seems to be no compelling reason to reject the common opinion of the early church on this matter.

C. Where Was Mark Written?

Early tradition does not unanimously agree about where Mark wrote his gospel, but it favors Rome. Other suggestions include Syria (specifically, Antioch), somewhere in the East, and Galilee. While certainty is impossible, Rome arises as the best alternative, granted the strength of the early tradition and the lack of any evidence to the contrary in the NT.

D. When Was Mark Written?

The majority of contemporary scholars date Mark in the mid to late 60s in the first century, but a decision between a date in the 50s and one in the 60s is impossible to make. We must be content with dating Mark sometime in the late 50s or the 60s.

E. To Whom Was Mark Written?

Mark is a self-effacing narrator. He tells his story with a minimum of editorial comments and says nothing about his intended audience. We must depend, then, on the early testimonies about Mark and on the character of the gospel itself.

Sources suggest that Mark wrote in Rome to Romans, primarily a Gentile Christian audience. Many of Mark's words or ways of saying things are derived from or suggestive of the Latin language; this is compatible with, if not conclusive for, a Roman audience. It seems clear that Mark writes to Gentiles because he translates Aramaic expressions, explains Jewish customs such as the washing of hands before eating (7:3–4), and shows interest in the cessation of the ritual elements in the Mosaic law (see 7:19; 12:32–34).

F. Why Was Mark Written?

Mark's purpose is much harder to determine, for he says nothing explicit about it. The content of Mark's gospel suggests at least four purposes:

1. Jesus. Mark is essentially "a passion narrative with an extended introduction" (Martin Kähler). It sets Jesus' miracle-working power (the focus in 1:16–8:26) beside his suffering and death (the focus in 8:27–16:8).
2. Discipleship. Mark correlates Jesus' predicted sufferings with the "cost of discipleship" (8:26–10:52). Jesus is the *suffering* Son

of God (15:39), and believers are to be *followers* of Jesus. Christians must walk the same road as Jesus — the way of humility, suffering, and if necessary, death (8:34).

3. Historical record. Mark provides Christian readers with a record of Jesus' deeds and words. This was becoming a great need in Mark's day as the original eyewitnesses such as Peter were beginning to pass from the scene.

4. Evangelism. Mark apparently wants to arm his Christian readers with a knowledge of the good news because (1) he focuses on Jesus' actions, (2) his structure is similar to early Christian evangelistic preaching (see below), and (3) he intends to write about "the good news" (1:1).

G. Is Mark 16:9–20 Authentic?

The majority of Greek manuscripts include the so-called long ending (16:9–20 in the KJV), which narrates several resurrection appearances of Jesus, his commissioning of the disciples, and his ascension. Modern English versions usually print verses 9–20 in the margin or with a notation. The arguments against this ending being original are very strong, so we (along with the great majority of contemporary scholars) do not think Mark wrote verses 9–20. Most likely, someone else composed this longer ending to supplement what was felt to be an inadequate ending to Mark's gospel.

Mark probably intended to end with verse 8. His gospel refrains from commenting on the significance of the history it narrates and instead lets the story speak for itself, forcing readers to discover the ultimate significance of much of the story of Jesus. A somewhat enigmatic ending to the gospel suits this strategy perfectly. The reader knows that Jesus has been raised (v. 6), but the confusion and astonishment of the women (v. 8) leave us wondering what it all means. That is just the question Mark wants us to ask and seek to answer.

H. What Does Mark Contribute to Our Understanding of the Faith?

1. The first gospel. Mark was the first to compose a gospel. By uniquely modifying the Greco-Roman style of literature called "biography," he created the style of literature called "gospel." He interweaves themes of Jesus' life and ministry to convey that Jesus of Nazareth (a real human) is the Son of God. By

reminding Christians that their salvation depends on the death and resurrection of Christ, Mark has inseparably tied Christian faith to the reality of historical events.

2. Structure. The sequence of Mark's gospel follows the same sequence revealed in the early church's preaching. Note the parallels between the preaching of Peter in Acts 10:36–40 and the structure of Mark in the following table.

Parallels between Peter's Preaching and Mark

Acts 10	Mark
"good news" (v. 36)	"the beginning of the good news" (1:1)
"God anointed Jesus of Nazareth with the Holy Spirit" (v. 38)	the coming of the Spirit on Jesus (1:10)
"beginning in Galilee" (v. 37)	the Galilean ministry (1:16–8:26)
"He went around doing good and healing all who were under the power of the devil" (v. 38)	Jesus' ministry focuses on healings and exorcisms
"We are witnesses of everything he did … in Jerusalem" (v. 39)	the ministry in Jerusalem (chs. 11–14)
"They killed him by hanging him on a cross" (v. 39)	focus on the death of Christ (ch. 15)
"God raised him from the dead on the third day" (v. 40)	"He has risen! He is not here" (16:6)

While Mark's sequence is to a considerable extent dictated by the actual course of events, his straightforward, action-oriented account preserves the sequence more clearly than do the other gospels. Mark's "preaching" structure helps readers understand the basic salvation events and prepares them to recite those events in their own evangelism.

3. Jesus' suffering. Mark's sequence also highlights its central structural divide: Peter's divinely given insight into the true nature of the man, Jesus of Nazareth (8:27–30). The first half

of Mark (1:1–8:26) leads up to this by emphasizing Jesus' miracles, and the second half (8:31–16:8) emphasizes Jesus' suffering and death. This combination of emphases reveals one of Mark's major purposes: Jesus is the *suffering* Son of God and can truly be understood only in terms of this suffering.

4. Discipleship. The twelve apostles figure very prominently in Mark and serve in general as a pattern for the disciples whom Mark addresses in his gospel. To be sure, the Twelve are not always presented as models to be emulated: their conspicuous failure is especially prominent in Mark (e.g., 6:52; 8:14–21; 14:32–42). Perhaps Mark implicitly wants to contrast the situation of the Twelve with that of Christian disciples at his time of writing: while the former sought to follow Jesus before the cross and the resurrection, the latter follow him with help from the powers of the new age of salvation that has dawned.

I. Questions for Review and Discussion

1. How is Mark's style and content different than Matthew's?
2. What is the relationship between Jesus' suffering and our discipleship?
3. What is significant about Mark's structure?

J. Recommended Resources

Introductory

Garland, David E. *Mark*. NIVAC. Grand Rapids: Zondervan, 1996.

Intermediate

Wessel, Walter W. "Mark." In *Matthew–Luke*. Rev. ed. EBC 9. Grand Rapids: Zondervan, 2010.

Advanced

Edwards, James R. *The Gospel According to Mark*. PNTC. Grand Rapids: Eerdmans, 2002.

chapter five

LUKE

A. What Is Luke About?

1. Prologue (1:1–4). Luke uniquely introduces his gospel with a formal prologue modeled along the lines of those found in Greek literature.

2. The births of John the Baptist and Jesus (1:5–2:52). Luke's "infancy narrative" focuses on the parallel miraculous births of John the Baptist and Jesus. Angels foretell their births (1:5–38), and Elizabeth and Mary, the related expectant mothers, meet (1:39–45). Mary's song of praise (1:46–56) is matched by that of John the Baptist's father, Zechariah (1:57–79). John "grew and became strong in spirit" (1:80), and Jesus "grew in wisdom and stature" (2:52 NIV). Luke records Jesus' birth in Bethlehem (2:1–7), the shepherds' visit (2:8–20), Jesus' presentation in the temple (2:21–40), and the one story we have of the boy Jesus (2:41–52).

3. Preparation for the ministry (3:1–4:13). Luke narrates the ministry of John the Baptist (3:1–20), Jesus' baptism (3:21–22), and Jesus' temptations (4:1–13). Like Matthew, Luke includes Jesus' genealogy, although their differences suggest that they trace different lines of descent (3:23–38).

4. The ministry of Jesus in Galilee (4:14–9:50)
   a. By starting with Jesus' sermon and rejection in Nazareth (4:16–30), Luke highlights Jesus' claim to be the Messiah predicted in Isaiah. He then records Jesus' typical activity: exorcism, healing, and proclaiming the kingdom of God (4:31–44).
   b. Luke contrasts the gathering of disciples with the opposition of Jewish authorities. Jesus brings about a miraculous catch

of fish and calls Simon to catch people (5:1 – 11). Then he heals a leper and a paralytic (5:12 – 26). Controversies arise over Jesus' association with "sinners" (5:27 – 32), the failure of Jesus' disciples to follow the Pharisees' guidelines for fasting (5:33 – 39), and the Sabbath (6:1 – 11). Jesus appoints the Twelve (6:12 – 16).

c. Luke presents Jesus' teaching about discipleship (6:17 – 49), two of Jesus' miracles (7:1 – 17), Jesus' teaching about John the Baptist (7:18 – 35), and a sinful woman's anointing of Jesus (7:36 – 50).

d. After a transitional interlude about women who followed Jesus (8:1 – 3), Luke highlights the importance of responding to God's word by narrating the parable of the sower (8:4 – 15), followed by Jesus' teaching about the lamp and about the need to listen (8:16 – 18), and Jesus' re-definition of his "family" in terms of hearing and doing God's word (8:19 – 21).

e. Luke features four examples of Jesus' characteristic miracles: a "nature" miracle, the stilling of the storm (8:22 – 25); an exorcism, the deliverance of the Gerasene demoniac (8:26 – 39); a healing, the curing of the woman with a hemorrhage; and a resurrection, the raising of Jairus's daughter (8:40 – 56).

f. Luke concludes his story of Jesus' ministry in Galilee by focusing on Jesus' identity and the nature of discipleship. Jesus sends out the Twelve (9:1 – 9), feeds the five thousand (9:10 – 17), and is recognized by Peter as the "Messiah of God" (9:18 – 27). Then comes Jesus' transfiguration (9:28 – 36), his healing of the boy with an evil spirit (9:37 – 45), and his teaching about discipleship (9:46 – 50).

5. Jesus' journey to Jerusalem (9:51 – 19:44). Luke focuses on Jesus' general movement toward Jerusalem to consummate his work.

a. Luke continues his focus on discipleship (9:51 – 11:13). After being rejected by some Samaritans, Jesus warns about the cost of following him (9:51 – 62). He sends out seventy-two preachers and rejoices at their report of success (10:1 – 24). In debate with a teacher of the law, Jesus uses the parable of the Good Samaritan to teach about true love for one's neighbor (10:25 – 37). A dispute between two sisters presents an occasion for Jesus to emphasize again the importance of listening to him (10:38–42). The unit concludes with teaching about the pattern and priority of prayer (11:5–13).

b. Jesus again addresses his opponents. He rebukes them for accusing him of exorcising demons in Satan's name (11:14–28), condemns his generation for failing to repent (11:29–32), cautions about the darkness of unbelief (11:33–36), and pronounces woes on his opponents (11:37–54). Opposition to him, he warns, is opposition to God himself (12:1–12). After using a parable to rebuke the arrogant rich (12:13–21), Jesus then addresses his followers, comforting them with the reminder of God's providential care (12:22–34) and emphasizing the need to discern the times and take appropriate action (12:35–13:9). He heals on the Sabbath, creating further controversy (13:10–17; 14:1–6), and teaches about the eventual spread of the kingdom and how it is to be entered (13:18–30). His lament over Jerusalem underscores the failure of so many Jews to respond to him (13:31–35), a point reiterated in both his warning about those who seek places of honor (14:7–14) and the parable of the great banquet (14:15–24). Again, he reminds his followers about the cost of discipleship (14:25–35; cf. 9:57–62).

c. The three parables about the "lost" sheep, coin, and son (15:1–32), reveal a theme of God's grace, while the parables of the dishonest manager and the rich man and Lazarus (16:1–31) present a theme of stewardship.

d. Luke includes a varied teaching of Jesus, most of it centered on the kingdom of God and the proper response to it (17:1–19:27). Jesus teaches about faithful service (17:1–10), commends a Samaritan's faith (17:11–19), and explains the nature of the kingdom and its final establishment (17:20–37). He calls for persistent faith and humility (18:1–17), warns about the dangers of wealth (18:18–30), predicts his passion (18:31–34), and heals a blind man (18:35–43). After encountering Zacchaeus, who manifests his repentance in the way he uses his wealth (19:1–10), Jesus tells a parable about the need to use the resources God puts at our disposal (19:11–27).

e. Jesus triumphantly enters Jerusalem (19:28–44)

6. Jesus in Jerusalem (19:45–21:38). In the days before his passion, Jesus cleanses the temple (19:45–46) and teaches (19:47–48; 21:37–38). Religious leaders question his authority (20:1–8), and he gives the parable of the wicked tenants (20:9–18). After a series of attempts to trap Jesus (20:19–44), he warns against the teachers of the law (20:45–47). Luke recounts the widow's gift (21:1–4) and Jesus' teaching about his coming again in glory (21:5–36).

7. Jesus' passion and resurrection (22:1–24:53)

   a. Luke sets the scene with Judas's betrayal of Jesus (22:1–6). He recounts the Last Supper and related teaching (22:7–38). The soldiers arrest Jesus in Gethsemane (22:39–54), Peter denies him, and the soldiers mock him (22:55–65). After all this, Jesus is put on trial before the Jewish Sanhedrin (22:66–71), Pilate (23:1–5), Herod Antipas (23:6–12), and again Pilate (23:13–25), only to be crucified and buried (23:26–56).

   b. After the empty tomb account (24:1–12), Luke focuses on the resurrected Jesus' conversation with a pair of disciples on the road to Emmaus (24:13–35). Jesus appears again before his disciples (24:36–49), and he ascends into heaven (24:50–53).

B. Who Wrote Luke?

Although anonymous, Luke and Acts probably never circulated without a name attached to them in some way. Evidence from within them and evidence from the early church indicates that the author is Luke, the doctor, Paul's "dear friend" (Col. 4:14). No one in the early church disputed the identification of Luke as the author, and the books use some medical language, which is compatible with this theory.

Luke was probably a Gentile who had strong sympathies for Judaism without becoming a convert (Col. 4:10–14). He was not an eyewitness to Jesus' ministry (Luke 1:1–4), and the "we" passages in the latter half of Acts suggest that he was Paul's companion. (See "Who Wrote Acts?" in ch. 7.)

C. Where Was Luke Written?

Early tradition claims that Luke was from Rome and wrote his gospel from Achaia. Later traditions name Rome as the place of writing.

Achaia is a reasonable conjecture, but insufficient evidence exists to link Luke's gospel definitely with any particular area.

D. When Was Luke Written?

The date of Luke's gospel closely intertwines with the dates of Mark and Acts.

1. If (as we have argued) Luke used Mark as a primary source for his gospel, then Luke must have been written later than Mark.
2. Luke must be earlier than Acts, since Acts presupposes the existence of Luke (Acts 1:1).

The two main options for when Luke was written are the A.D. 60s and between A.D. 75 and 85; we prefer the former. The only really significant argument for dating Luke after 70 is the (unconvincing) argument that Mark must be dated in the mid-60s at the earliest. But if Mark is dated in the late 50s or early 60s, then Luke could well have been written in the mid- or late 60s.

E. To Whom Was Luke Written?

Luke addresses his gospel to Theophilus. This might have been the individual's name, or Luke might be using an alias to guard the person's true identity. By calling him "most excellent," Luke may also imply that Theophilus was a person of rank, perhaps a Roman aristocrat (cf. Acts 24:3; 26:25). He was probably a recent convert to the faith (Luke 1:4), and he may have financed Luke's research and writing.

It is almost certain, however, that Luke had a wider reading public in view, primarily those with a Gentile background. Like the other gospels, Luke was not so much written to a specific location as to a specific kind of reader.

F. Why Was Luke Written?

Luke writes so that Theophilus "may know the certainty of the things" he has "been taught" (1:4). Luke wants Theophilus and other converts like him to be certain about the ultimate significance of what God has done in Christ. Why should they think that Christianity is the one "right" religion out of all the religious and philosophical alternatives in the Greco-Roman and Jewish world? Why should they continue to believe that God has revealed himself decisively in Jesus of Nazareth? Luke intends to answer these questions and strengthen the faith of converts.

G. How Does Luke Compare with Matthew and Mark?

Luke's gospel is the longest book in the NT. Like Matthew, it follows the basic outline of Jesus' ministry established by Mark: preparation for the ministry, ministry in Galilee, movement to Jerusalem, passion, and resurrection. However, Luke introduces many more modifications to this basic sequence than does Matthew. Especially striking is the amount of space he devotes to Jesus' movement to Jerusalem. Occupying one chapter in Mark (10) and two in Matthew (19–20), this section accounts for almost ten chapters in Luke (9:51–19:27). Luke makes room for this expansion by abbreviating the Galilean phase of the ministry (Luke 4:14–9:17, compared to Mark 1:14–8:26; Matt. 4:12–16:12).

Luke also introduces a significant amount of material not found in any other gospel, including famous parables such as the Good Samaritan (10:25–37), the Prodigal Son (15:11–32), and the Shrewd Manager (16:1–9). Only Luke records Jesus' encounter with Zacchaeus (19:1–10), his raising of a widow's son at Nain (7:11–17), and his words on the cross asking God to forgive his executioners (23:34) and assuring the dying thief of entrance into Paradise (23:43).

H. What Is the Relationship between Luke and Acts?

The prologues to Luke and Acts leave no doubt that a relationship exists. The same man — Theophilus — is addressed in each, and the "former book" mentioned in Acts 1:1 is undoubtedly Luke's gospel.

Some insist that Luke and Acts form one book ("Luke-Acts") that was divided into two volumes because a single papyrus scroll could not hold both. Virtually all scholars today agree that the same person wrote both books, and most also find a considerable degree of unity in their themes. Both books show how God has acted in history to fulfill his promises to Israel and to create a worldwide body of believers drawn from both Jews and Gentiles. The focus on Jerusalem in both Luke and Acts conveys this movement. Luke's gospel especially emphasizes the movement *toward* Jerusalem (e.g., 9:51; 13:33; 17:11), while Acts describes a movement *away* from Jerusalem. Other shared themes include salvation, the Holy Spirit's activity, and the power of God's word.

On the other hand, the literary style of Luke's gospel is biographical, but Acts is historical. Thus, we should probably consider Luke and Acts to be two separate books that stand in close relationship to each other. While Luke almost certainly had both books in mind when he began to write, we should consider each on its own when it comes to the question of style of literature, structure, purpose, and, to some extent, theology.

I. What Does Luke Contribute to Our Understanding of the Faith?

1. Survey. Luke's sweeping historical survey starts with Jesus' conception and birth and ends with his ascension. In between, he includes many stories and teachings of Jesus not found in the other gospels.
2. God's plan. What happens in Jesus' birth, life, death, and resurrection happens because God is working out a plan that he had set in place long ago and revealed in the OT. Certain events *must* occur, especially Jesus' death on the cross (9:22; 17:25; 22:37; 24:7, 44).
3. Salvation. Luke's central theme is God's plan to provide salvation for the world (19:10). In Jesus, God comes to his people as their Savior. He rescues the lost by providing for the forgiveness of sins (e.g., 1:77; 5:17–26; 7:48–50; 19:1–10; 24:46–47).
4. Gentiles. Luke by no means ignores Jews, but he emphasizes Gentiles as ultimate recipients of God's salvation (cf. 4:25–27; 7:1–10; 10:30–37; 17:16). This prepares the way for the inclusion of Gentiles in the people of God (see Acts).
5. Outcasts. Jesus is concerned for and constantly interacts with the outcasts of Jewish society: the poor (e.g., 1:46–55; 4:18; 6:20–23; 7:22; 10:21–22; 14:13, 21–24; 16:19–31; 21:1–4), "sinners" (e.g., those who did not abide by all the pharisaic rituals—5:27–32; 7:28, 30, 34, 36–50; 15:1–2; 19:7), and women (7:36–50; 8:1–3, 48; 10:38–42; 13:10–17; 24:1–12). Luke often pictures those on the margins of society as particularly responsive to Jesus' message. He warns both explicitly and implicitly about the importance of putting aside the entanglements of this world in order to embrace freely and wholeheartedly the message of the kingdom. This message has been seized on by some theologians, especially liberation theologians, to

argue that the poor and the oppressed are specially favored by God, while the rich and powerful are rejected. Passages such as Jesus' blessing on the poor and his corresponding "woe" on the rich (6:20, 24) could suggest just such a view. But we must recall that Jesus uses the language of "poor" and "rich" against the background of the Old Testament, where these terms held not only economic but social and spiritual significance. The "poor" to whom Jesus refers do not just lack money; they also depend on God to meet their needs. The "rich" he speaks of do not just have money; they also use their wealth and power to oppress the poor. Translation of Luke's categories of "poor" and "rich" into our cultural categories must take account of these nuances.

6. Stewardship. Another facet of Luke's socioeconomic interest is his emphasis on the need for disciples to reveal their sincerity in following Jesus by the way they handle their money (3:10 – 14; 12:13 – 21; 16:1 – 13; 16:19 – 31; 19:1 – 10).

J. Questions for Review and Discussion

1. Why did Luke write his gospel?
2. What is distinct about Luke compared to the other gospels?
3. What is the relationship between Luke and Acts?
4. What is Luke's central theme?

K. Recommended Resources

Introductory

Bock, Darrell L. *Luke*. NIVAC. Grand Rapids: Zondervan, 1996.

Intermediate

Bock, Darrell L. *Luke*. IVPNTC. Downers Grove: InterVarsity Press, 1994.

Liefeld, Walter L., and David W. Pao. "Luke." Pages 19 – 355 in *Luke – Acts*. Rev. ed. EBC 10. Grand Rapids: Zondervan, 2007.

Stein, Robert H. *Luke*. NAC 24. Nashville: Broadman & Holman, 1992.

Advanced

Marshall, I. Howard. *Luke: Historian and Theologian*. Downers Grove: InterVarsity Press, 1970.

chapter six

JOHN

A. What Is John About?

1. Prologue (1:1–18). The Word, God's own equal and God's own self, becomes a human being.

2. Jesus discloses himself in word and deed (1:19–10:42)

    a. As a prelude to Jesus' public ministry, John the Baptist witnesses concerning Jesus (1:19–34), who gains his first disciples (1:35–51).

    b. Jesus' early ministry consists of signs, works, and words (2:1–4:54). He changes water into wine (2:1–11) and cleanses the temple (2:12–17), which he replaces (2:18–22). The inadequate faith of many who trust him at this juncture (2:23–25) sets the stage for the exchange between Jesus and Nicodemus (3:1–15) and what appears to be John's extended comment (3:16–21). John describes John the Baptist's continuing witness concerning Jesus (3:22–30) and again follows it with commentary (3:31–36). On his way to Galilee, Jesus stops in Samaria and leads both a Samaritan woman and many of her countrymen to faith in himself (4:1–42), and in Galilee he heals an official's son (4:43–54).

    c. John recounts more of Jesus' signs, works, and words, but now in the context of rising opposition (5:1–7:53). Jesus heals a paralytic on the Sabbath (5:1–15), which triggers some opposition that Jesus quickly transforms into a question about the nature of his sonship to the Father (5:16–30). After his central claims about himself, he names other witnesses concerning himself (5:31–47). Jesus' feeding five thousand (6:1–15) and walking on water (6:16–21) introduce his bread of life discourse, where Jesus claims that he is himself the true manna, the living bread that must be eaten (6:22–58). This gives rise to more hesitations: opinion is divided over him, and even some of his disciples turn against him, while he retains the initiative in determining who truly are his followers (6:59–71). Skepticism and uncertainty regarding him continue, even among members of his own family (7:1–13). This means that the first round of exchanges at the Feast of Tabernacles (7:14–44) is frankly confrontational and leads to the first organized opposition from the Jewish authorities (7:45–52).

d. Jesus' signs, works, and words climax in the context of radical confrontation (8:12–10:42). The second round of exchanges at the Feast of Tabernacles ends with Jesus telling the authorities that they are children of the devil, while he himself is none less than the "I am" — and this sparks a futile attempt to stone him to death (8:12–59). Jesus' healing of the man born blind allows no connection between sin and the man's condition and climaxes by denouncing those who think they see (9:1–41). The Jews predictably react when Jesus presents himself as the good shepherd of the sheep, making his own messianic flock the people of God (10:1–21). At the Feast of Dedication, Jesus' claims to be both Messiah and Son of God engender open opposition, prompting Jesus to make a strategic retreat accompanied by growing numbers of believers (10:22–42).

3. Transition (11:1–12:50)

a. The story of Lazarus' death and resurrection is a foreshadowing that anticipates Jesus' death and resurrection (11:1–44), and it directly leads to the decision to kill Jesus (11:45–54).

b. This section occurs during the "Jewish Passover" (11:55–57). Anticipating the death of the true Passover lamb, Mary anoints Jesus, displaying sacrificial love for him — the only kind of any value (12:1–11). The triumphal entry announces Jesus' kingship, but the ominous signs are already present that this kingship will be unlike any other (12:12–19). The arrival of the Gentiles triggers Jesus' announcement of the dawning "hour" of his death and exaltation (12:20–36).

     c. Jesus reveals the nature and inevitability of unbelief (12:37-50).

4. Jesus discloses himself in his cross and exaltation (13:1–20:31).

     a. Instead of preserving any report of the institution of the Lord's Supper, John recalls how Jesus washed his disciples' feet (13:1–17). Jesus predicts his betrayal, leaving no doubt that he remains in charge of his own destiny, in submission to his Father's will (13:18–30).

     b. Jesus' so-called farewell discourse explains the significance of his death and exaltation *before* the sign itself takes place (13:31–16:33). Jesus also explains the role of the promised Holy Spirit, whom Jesus gives to believers after his exaltation.

     c. Jesus prays for his own glorification (17:1–5), for his disciples (17:6–19), for those who will later believe (17:20–23), and, climactically, for all believers to be perfected and see his glory (17:24–26).

     d. Jesus' trial and passion emphasize the nature of his kingship (18:1–19:42).

     e. John's account of Jesus' resurrection includes several resurrection appearances and concisely states his gospel's purpose (20:1–31).

5. Epilogue (21:1–25). John not only ties up several loose ends (e.g., Peter's restoration to service) but in symbolic ways points to the church's growth and diversity of gifts and callings. It appropriately ends with a tribute to Jesus' greatness (21:25).

B. Who Wrote John?

Like the Synoptic Gospels, the fourth gospel does not explicitly assert its author's name. As far as we can prove, the title "According to John" was attached to it as soon as the four gospels began to circulate together as "the fourfold gospel." In part, no doubt, this was to distinguish it from the rest of the collection, but it may have served as the title from the beginning.

In short, the most straightforward reading of the evidence is still the traditional one: it is highly probable that John the son of Zebedee wrote the fourth gospel. This makes no difference whatsoever to the book's authority (after all, Luke's gospel does not claim to be by an eyewitness), but it does affect how we think about the book's background and purpose.

C. Where Was John Written?

The fourth gospel does not specify where John wrote it. Four places are commonly proposed: Alexandria, Antioch, Palestine, and Ephesus. The traditional view is that John wrote it in Ephesus, and no other location has the support of the church fathers. If John wrote it while residing in Ephesus, then perhaps he prepared it for readers in this general part of the empire, while still hoping for the widest possible circulation.

D. When Was John Written?

Almost any date between about A.D. 55 and 95 is possible. None of the arguments is entirely convincing; however, if a date for the writing of the fourth gospel must be suggested, we may very tentatively advance A.D. 80–85. One of many reasons for this is to allow some time before John wrote his three letters, which combat an incipient form of Gnosticism and respond in part to a gnostic misunderstanding of the fourth gospel. (See ch. 23.)

E. Why and to Whom Was John Written?

The proper place to begin is with John's own purpose statement (20:30–31). While he clearly wrote 1 John to encourage Christians (1 John 5:13), the purpose for his gospel seems to be evangelistic. This impression is confirmed by the solid evidence that the first purpose clause in John 20:31 should be rendered "that you may believe the Christ, the Son of God, is Jesus." Thus, the fundamental question the fourth gospel addresses is not "Who is Jesus?" but "Who is the Messiah, the Christ, the Son of God?" In its context, the latter is a question of identity, not of kind: that is, the question "Who is the Christ?" should not here be taken to mean "What kind of Christ are you talking about?" but "So you claim to know who the Christ is. Prove it, then: Who is he?"

Christians would not ask that kind of question because they already knew the answer. The most likely people to ask that sort of question would be Jews and Jewish proselytes who know what "the Christ" means, have some sort of messianic expectation, and are perhaps in dialogue with Christians and want to know more. In short, John's gospel not only is evangelistic in its purpose but aims in particular to evangelize Jews dispersed outside of Palestine as well as Jewish proselytes.

F. How Does John Compare with the Synoptic Gospels?

Differences

1. John omits many of Jesus' words and works that are characteristic of the Synoptic Gospels: narrative parables, the account of the transfiguration, the record of the institution of the Lord's Supper, and many of Jesus' more concise sayings.

2. John omits themes central to the Synoptic Gospels, especially the theme of the kingdom of God (also referred to as the kingdom of heaven).

3. John includes a substantial amount of material not mentioned in the Synoptic Gospels: nearly all the material in John 1 – 5, Jesus' frequent visits to Jerusalem and the events that take place there, and the resurrection of Lazarus are all exclusive to John's gospel, as are Jesus' *explicit* identification with God (1:1, 18; 20:28) and his series of "I am" statements (e.g., 6:35; 8:12, 28, 58; 15:1 – 5). John also includes extended dialogues and discourses not found elsewhere in the gospels.

4. Doubtless some of this can be accounted for by the different geographic focus: John reports far more of Jesus' ministry in the south (Judea and Samaria), while the Synoptic Gospels focus on the north (Galilee). However, one cannot legitimately reduce all distinctions to questions of geography.

Similarities

It appears likely that John had read Mark, Luke, and possibly even Matthew; however, it cannot be proven that John directly borrowed from the Synoptic Gospels (in the sense that Matthew and Luke likely borrowed from Mark).

1. Parallel incidents include the Spirit's anointing of Jesus as testified by John the Baptist (1:32), the contrast between John the Baptist's baptism with water and the Messiah's anticipated baptism with the Spirit (1:23), the feeding of the five thousand (6:1 – 15), and Jesus' walking on water (6:16 – 21).

2. Many sayings are at least partially parallel (4:35, 44; 5:29; 10:14 – 15; 12:39 – 40; and many more).

3. More significant yet are the subtle parallels: both John and the Synoptic Gospels describe a Jesus given to colorful metaphors

and proverbs, many drawn from the world of nature (e.g., 4:37; 5:19–20a; 8:35; 9:4; 11:9–10; 10:1ff.; 12:24; 15:1–16; 16:21). All four gospels depict Jesus with a unique sense of sonship to his heavenly Father; all of them note the distinctive authority Jesus displays in his teaching; all of them show Jesus referring to himself as the Son of Man, a title used neither by nor toward anyone else.

4. Even more impressive are the many places where John and the Synoptics represent an *interlocking* tradition, that is, where they mutually reinforce or explain each other without necessarily borrowing from each other.

   a. John explains several events from the Synoptic Gospels. For example, the charge that Jesus had threatened the destruction of the temple (Mark 14:58; 15:29) finds its only adequate explanation in John 2:19. Mark gives no reason as to why the Jewish authorities should bother bringing Jesus to Pilate; John provides the reason (18:31). Only John explains why Peter can be placed within the high priest's courtyard (18:15–18; cf. Mark 14:54, 66–72).

   b. Conversely, numerous features in John are explained by details reported only in the Synoptic Gospels. For instance, in John 18–19 the trial plunges so quickly into the Roman court that it is difficult to see just what judicial action the Jews have taken, if any, to precipitate this trial; the Synoptics provide the answer.

G. Is John 7:53–8:11 Authentic?

The story of the woman caught in adultery (7:53–8:11) was almost certainly not originally part of John's gospel. Modern English versions are right to rule it off from the rest of the text or to relegate it to a footnote. These verses are absent from virtually all early Greek manuscripts that have come down to us.

H. What Does John Contribute to Our Understanding of the Faith?

John's thought is so wonderfully integrated that attempts to compartmentalize it by itemizing its components are destined in some measure to misrepresent it. Nevertheless, among John's more important contributions are the following:

1. Enriching perspective. By telling the same story from another angle, John adds a stereoscopic depth to the picture of Jesus that we might not gain from the Synoptic Gospels alone.

2. Son of God. Fundamental to all else that is said of him, Jesus is peculiarly the Son of God, or simply the Son. He is functionally subordinate to the Father and does and says only those things the Father gives him to do and say, but he does *everything* that the Father does (5:19ff.). Jesus discloses nothing more and nothing less than the words and deeds of God.

3. Cross. Despite the heavy emphasis on Jesus as the one who reveals his Father, salvation does not come (as in Gnosticism) merely by revelation. All the movement of the plot is toward the cross and resurrection. The cross is not merely a revelatory moment: it is the victory of the Lamb of God (1:29, 35), the life that is given for the world (6:25–58), the death of the shepherd for his sheep (10:11–18), the sacrifice of one man for his nation (11:50–52), and the triumph of the obedient Son, who by his death gives his life, peace, joy, and Spirit (14–16).

4. Tension between "already" and "not yet." All the major New Testament writings display the tension that (1) God's promised "last days" have *already* arrived in Jesus' ministry, death, resurrection, and exaltation, and (2) the fullness of hope is *not yet* here but still to come. Different authors display the tension in different ways, and John's distinctive emphasis is bound up with his use of the "present and future" theme (e.g., 2:4; 7:6). The hour "is coming and has now come" (4:23; 5:25). Jesus has given his peace, but in this world we will have trouble (16:33). In the wake of Jesus' exaltation and his gift of the Spirit, we can possess eternal life right now, but this is never at the expense of all future hope (5:28–30).

5. Holy Spirit. By giving the Spirit, Jesus introduces what is characteristic under the new covenant (3:5; 7:37–39). Jesus gives the Spirit, the Counselor, in consequence of his death and exaltation (14–16). The elements of what came to be called the doctrine of the Trinity find their clearest articulation in John's gospel.

6. Use of the Old Testament. Although John does not cite the OT as frequently as does Matthew, for example, his use of the OT is characterized by an extraordinary number of allusions, and above all by his insistence that Jesus in certain respects replaces

revered figures and institutions from the old covenant (e.g. temple, vine, tabernacle, serpent, Passover).

7. Misunderstandings. No gospel better preserves the ways in which Jesus was misunderstood by his contemporaries (including his own disciples) until after his exaltation. This is significant for reflecting on the relation between the old and new covenants.

8. People of God. John devotes much attention to the concept of what it means to belong to the people of God. Although there is nothing on church order per se, there is much on the election, life, origin, nature, witness, suffering, fruit-bearing, prayer, love, and unity of the people of God.

9. Vocabulary. John in certain respects provides greater depth than do the Synoptic Gospels, but on relatively restricted topics. This is a major reason that he uses a smaller vocabulary, using certain words and expressions repeatedly (e.g., believe, love, world, send, Father).

10. God's sovereignty and human responsibility. John repeatedly explores the complexities that bind together election, faith, and the function of signs. If faith bursts forth in consequence of what is revealed in the signs, then signs legitimately serve as a basis for faith (e.g., 10:38). Yet in contrast, people are rebuked for their dependence on signs (4:48), because it is a better faith that hears and believes rather than sees and believes (20:29). In the last analysis, faith turns on sovereign election by the Son (15:16) and on being part of the gift from the Father to the Son (6:37–44). This truth is at the heart of a book that is persistently evangelistic.

I. Questions for Review and Discussion

1. How does John compare to the Synoptic Gospels?
2. What was John's purpose for writing this gospel?
3. What contributions of John's gospel are most striking to you?

J. Recommended Resources

Introductory

Carson, D. A. *The Farewell Discourse and Final Prayer of Jesus: An Exposition of John 14–17.* Grand Rapids: Baker, 1980. Reprinted as *Jesus and His Friends.* Carlisle: Paternoster, 1995.

The Gospel of John. DVD. Directed by Philip Saville. Burbank, CA: Buena Vista Home Entertainment, 2003. (This is a three-hour film presenting John's gospel. The script follows the Good News Translation verbatim. The film is classy, tasteful, modest, creative, thought-provoking, instructional, edifying, reverent, and accessible.)

Köstenberger, Andreas J. *Encountering John: The Gospel in Historical, Literary, and Theological Perspective*. Grand Rapids: Baker, 1999.

Intermediate

Blomberg, Craig L. *The Historical Reliability of John's Gospel: Issues and Commentary*. Downers Grove: InterVarsity Press, 2001.

Advanced

Carson, D. A. *Divine Sovereignty and Human Responsibility*. Atlanta: John Knox, 1981. (This is a revision of Carson's PhD dissertation.)

———. *The Gospel According to John*. PNTC. Grand Rapids: Eerdmans, 1991.

Keener, Craig S. *The Gospel of John: A Commentary*. 2 vols. Peabody: Hendrickson, 2003.

chapter seven

ACTS

A. What Is Acts About?

Acts is a whirlwind tour of three decades of church history. The story moves from Jerusalem to Judea, Samaria, Syria, Cyprus, many cities in Asia Minor, Macedonia, Greece, and finally, Rome. It witnesses everything from preaching and miracles to jailbreaks and shipwrecks. Two men in particular dominate the story: Peter (prominent in chs. 1–12) and Paul (prominent in chs. 13–28). The book is divided into six parts marked off by key summary statements highlighting the growth of God's word or church (6:7; 9:31; 12:24; 16:5; 19:20).

1. Foundations for the church and its mission (1:1–2:41) followed by the church in Jerusalem (2:42–6:7). The church and its mission are rooted in the acts and words of Jesus, who prepares the apostles for the coming of the Spirit and charges them with their worldwide missionary mandate (1:1–8). Luke describes Jesus' ascension into heaven (1:9–11; cf. Luke 24:50–51), the choosing of Matthias to replace Judas (Acts 1:12–26), the coming of the Spirit on the Day of Pentecost (2:1–13), and the first missionary sermon (2:14–41).

   Luke lists characteristics of the early church in Jerusalem (2:42–47) and describes Peter's healing of a crippled man in the temple precincts (3:1–10), a public miracle that gains Peter a hearing for another missionary sermon (3:13–26). Opposition arises from the Sanhedrin, but Peter and John boldly resist its request that they cease speaking "in the name of Jesus" (4:1–22). The church as a whole, infused with the power of the Spirit, follows the lead of the apostles, preaching the word of God boldly after having prayed that God would grant them such

53

opportunity (4:23–31). But all is not perfect: the married couple Ananias and Sapphira lie about their participation in the early community's voluntary sharing program (4:32–37), and God swiftly judges them (5:1–11). The apostles' popular healing and preaching ministry (5:12–16) again sparks opposition from the Jewish leaders, and again the apostles are arrested and brought before the Sanhedrin; Gamaliel, an important rabbi of his day, counsels moderation, and the apostles are released (5:17–42). In order to give themselves fully to the preaching of the word, the apostles appoint seven men to regulate the distribution of food among the community (6:1–6). Luke summarizes that in this way "the word of God spread" (6:7).

2. Wider horizons for the church: Stephen, Samaria, and Saul (6:8–9:31). To this point in the story, Luke has portrayed the early believers as loyal, if somewhat unusual, Jews. He now shows the church beginning to strain the bounds of traditional Judaism. Stephen is falsely accused of speaking against the temple and the law (6:8–15). When brought before the Sanhedrin to answer charges about his teaching, Stephen boldly uses a sketch of Israel's history to suggest that God's revelation cannot be confined to one place and to charge the Sanhedrin members themselves with resisting the Holy Spirit (7:1–53). The Sanhedrin condemns and stones Stephen (7:54–60).

Stephen's radical stance sparks opposition to the young Christian movement, and "all except the apostles" are forced to leave Jerusalem (8:1–3). Philip then brings the gospel to Samaria, a territory to the north of Judea inhabited by people considered by most Jews to be renegade Jews at best. The Samaritans believe Philip's message, and Peter and John are sent to confirm that the Samaritans have indeed been accepted into the kingdom of God (8:4–25). Philip, directed by an angel, travels south, where God uses him to convert an Ethiopian court official (8:26–40). Finally, Luke recounts the conversion and early ministry of the one chosen by God to be the pioneer in the mission to the Gentiles: Saul of Tarsus (9:1–30). Luke closes with a summary statement of the church's growth (9:31).

3. Peter and the first Gentile convert (9:32–12:24). Luke describes Peter's role in opening the way for Gentiles to become Christians. After Peter performs miracles in Lydda and Joppa (9:32–43), God uses Peter to bring Cornelius, a Gentile Roman

soldier, into the church. Through visions and the Spirit's direct command, God brings Cornelius and Peter together (10:1–23). At Cornelius's house, God's sovereign action interrupts Peter's preaching of the gospel: God gives the Spirit to Cornelius in so evident a manner that Peter has to recognize that God had truly accepted a Gentile into his church (10:24–48). This enables Peter to reassure Jewish-Christian skeptics in Jerusalem about the reality of Cornelius's conversion (11:1–18). The mixture of Jews and Gentiles in the church at Antioch necessitates that believers in Jesus be given a new name: Christians (11:19–30). Peter miraculously escapes from prison (12:1–19), and an angel of the Lord kills Herod Agrippa I, who had initiated the persecution that led to Peter's arrest (12:20–23). Luke again closes with a transitional summary: "the word of God continued to increase and spread" (12:24).

4. Paul turns to the Gentiles (12:25–16:5). Paul dominates the remainder of the book, as God uses Paul to pioneer an extensive gospel ministry to Gentiles.

   a. God's Spirit leads the vibrant church at Antioch to send Paul, along with Barnabas and John Mark, on the first missionary journey (12:25–13:3). In Cyprus, a Roman official is converted (13:4–12). In Pisidian Antioch, Paul's ministry illustrates a typical pattern: he preaches to Jews in the synagogue, they reject the gospel, Paul and his companions turn directly to the Gentiles, and then Jewish persecution forces them to move on (13:13–52). They minister in Iconium (14:1–7); Lystra, where Paul is stoned (14:8–20); and Derbe, planting churches in each city and strengthening the new believers as they retrace their steps again to the coast (14:21–28).

   b. Upon arriving back in Antioch, the missionaries are confronted with a serious dispute about their outreach to the Gentiles. A council convened in Jerusalem to discuss the matter endorses the law-free offer of the gospel to the Gentiles, a decision that is of vital importance in establishing the character of the church and enabling its further growth (15:1–29). Paul and Barnabas bring the good news back to Antioch and begin planning a new missionary trip, but their inability to agree about taking along John Mark, who had turned for home before the first journey was complete, leads them to split. Barnabas takes Mark with him back to Cyprus and Paul takes Silas with him overland to Syria, Cilicia, and on to the churches established on the first journey (15:30–41). Here Paul also recruits Timothy for the cause (16:1–4). Again Luke concludes, "the churches were strengthened in the faith and grew daily in numbers" (16:5).

5. Further penetration into the Gentile world (16:6–19:20). God's Spirit directs Paul step-by-step to take the gospel into Macedonia (16:6–10). In Philippi, the Lord opens Lydia's heart (16:11–15), and an exorcism temporarily lands Paul and Silas in jail; then God miraculously rescues them, and Paul uses his Roman citizenship to secure his release (16:16–40). Paul and Silas move on to Thessalonica, but persecution forces them to Berea (17:1–9) and Athens (17:10–15). In Athens, Paul preaches to a sophisticated, skeptical, Gentile audience on so-called Mars Hill (17:16–34).

The results in Athens seem to be meager, so Paul spends a year and a half in Corinth, preaching, defending himself before the Roman official Gallio, and enlisting the Roman Jewish couple Priscilla and Aquila in the work of the gospel (18:1–17). The three leave Corinth for Ephesus, where Paul leaves Priscilla and Aquila while he proceeds on to Caesarea, Antioch, and the churches of southern Asia Minor (18:18–23). Meanwhile in Ephesus, Priscilla and Aquila establish more firmly in the faith the gifted young man Apollos (18:24–28). Paul then ministers in Ephesus for two and a half years, converting some disciples of John the Baptist, preaching in the synagogue and a lecture hall, working miracles, and confronting the demonism for which the city was known (19:1–19). Again Luke summarizes, "In this way the word of the Lord spread widely and grew in power" (19:20).

6. On to Rome (19:21–28:31). Paul's third missionary journey continues, and he is determined to go to Rome (19:21–22), a resolve that drives Luke's story from this point on. Paul leaves Ephesus only after a riot forces him to go (19:23–41). He revisits the churches in Macedonia and Greece and decides to return to Judea by the same route because of a plot against his life (20:1–6). On his way back, he stops to preach in Troas and meets in Miletus with the elders of the Ephesian church (20:7–38). He arrives in Jerusalem via Tyre and Caesarea with

warnings about his impending arrest in Jerusalem ringing in his ears (21:1–16). The warning quickly becomes reality.

Paul's willingness to "fly his Jewish flag" for the sake of the Jewish Christians in Jerusalem by paying for, and joining in, some purification rites in the temple backfires (21:17–26). Certain Jews think that Paul has brought Gentiles into the temple with him, and the ensuing riot forces the Romans to intervene (21:27–36). Paul is arrested but is allowed to address the crowd before being taken away (21:37–22:22). His Roman citizenship again stands him in good stead, and he is allowed to state his case before the Jewish Sanhedrin (22:30–23:10). The Lord assures Paul that he will live to testify about his faith in Rome, despite a plot of the Jews to kill him (23:11–15). Because of this threat, Paul is moved to Caesarea, where he defends himself before the Roman governor Felix (23:16–24:27). After Paul has languished in prison in Caesarea for two years, Festus replaces Felix, and Paul forces the issue by appealing to Caesar to hear his case (25:1–12). Before leaving, however, Paul again defends himself before Festus and his guests, King Agrippa II and his sister Bernice (25:13–26:32). A severe storm interrupts Paul's journey to Rome, stranding Paul and his sailing companions for three months on the island of Malta (27:1–28:10). Paul finally arrives in Rome, where he is able to live in his own house, under guard, and preach the gospel freely (28:11–31). Luke's tour of the gospel's expansion ends with Paul in Rome for two years under house arrest.

B. Who Wrote Acts?

While both Luke and Acts are, strictly speaking, anonymous, the author of these books is almost certainly Luke. One line of evidence for this is a group of four passages in Acts (16:8–17; 20:5–15; 21:1–18; 27:1–28:16) in which the author shifts from his usual third-person narration (e.g., *he, him, they, them*) to a first-person plural narration (e.g., *we, us*). The natural reading of these passages is that the author of Acts was present during the events he narrates in these passages and that he kept a diary or itinerary report that he incorporates into Acts. The author could not have been any of the companions of Paul who are mentioned in these passages, and since the author accompanied Paul to Rome and was probably with him during Paul's two-year house arrest, we might expect Paul to mention him in the letters he wrote during that period of time: Colossians, Philemon, Ephesians, and, perhaps, Philippians. The companions Paul names are Mark, Jesus Justus, Epaphras, Demas, Luke, Tychicus, Timothy, Aristarchus, and Epaphroditus.

Evidence outside Acts takes over at this point and singles out Luke from the list of possible candidates. The unanimous opinion of the early church is that Paul's companion and the author of Acts was Luke "the beloved physician." Unfortunately, we do not know very much about his background. (See "Who Wrote Luke?" in ch. 5.)

C. When Was Acts Written?

Although most scholars now date Acts in the A.D. 80s or a bit later, the reasons for a late date are unconvincing and based on invalid assumptions. A date in the mid-60s fits the evidence much better.

Some think that the abrupt ending of Acts is solid evidence of its date in the early 60s. They argue that the simplest and most natural explanation for the abrupt ending is that Luke finished writing the book when Paul had been under house arrest in Rome for two years. The abrupt ending, however, does not point *conclusively* to the date of its writing or publication.

D. To Whom and Why Was Acts Written?

Acts, like the gospel of Luke, is addressed to Theophilus (1:1), who probably paid to publish Luke's literary effort. But it is almost certain that Luke had a broader audience than one individual in mind.

Luke wrote Acts with multiple purposes:

1. Instill certainty. If Luke's gospel and Acts are two volumes of the same writing, then Luke 1:4 applies to Acts as well, namely, to communicate the "certainty of the things you have been taught."
2. Conciliate Jews and Gentiles. It is wrong to view Acts as *fabricating* a harmony between Peter and Paul, as if the two apostles were actually doctrinally opposed to one another. But Luke may have known of continuing tensions between Jewish and Gentile Christians and wanted to show that Peter and Paul were in essential agreement over the basics of the faith.
3. Evangelize and defend Christianity. Luke paraphrases several evangelistic speeches, recounts miracles by the early preachers, and spends nearly one-fourth of the book detailing Paul's trials and defenses (chs. 22–28). He likely intends to evangelize unbe-

lievers and defend Christianity in the eyes of skeptical Romans. Or perhaps he wanted to help new converts from a Roman background to better understand the relationship between their new faith and their Roman political and social identity. Many features of Luke-Acts imply a Gentile Christian audience.

4. Edify Christians. Luke's *primary* objective is to edify Christians by recounting how God's plan is fulfilled in Jesus and continues to unfold in early church history. Perhaps Luke's intended readers are former God-fearers, that is, Gentiles like Cornelius (Acts 10) who had strong sympathies for Judaism without becoming converts. Such people would have wondered about the place of Christianity (especially as opposed to Judaism) within the flurry of religious and philosophical options available in their Greco-Roman world. Luke edifies such Christians by describing Christianity's historical foundation and showing that the church is the culmination of biblical history. God's salvation was revealed in, and made available through, Jesus Christ, who entrusted the message of that salvation to his apostles. Through the Holy Spirit's empowering and directing, Christians have now brought that message of salvation to "the ends of the earth" (1:8; 13:47).

E. What Style of Literature Is Acts?

The book we know as the Acts of the Apostles belongs with Luke's gospel as the second volume in a history of Christian beginnings. The word "Acts" denoted a recognized type of writing in the ancient world, namely, books that described the great deeds of people or cities. Since Acts narrates the founding events of the church and ascribes most of them to apostles, the title is not inappropriate. Yet, judging from Luke's own emphases, he may have preferred a title such as "The Acts of the Holy Spirit" or "What Jesus Continued to Do and Teach" (see 1:1). Regardless, "acts" was not the name of a technical style of literature. Most scholars agree that Acts' style of literature is "history" (in contrast to Luke's gospel, which is "biography").

F. What Does Acts Contribute to Our Understanding of the Faith?

1. Reliable history. Acts claims to narrate actual historical events regarding the church's founding and growth. This history is indispensable because without it, we would know nothing of the

pouring out of the Spirit at Pentecost, Stephen's martyrdom, the life of the early Jerusalem church, and how the gospel first came to Samaritans and Gentiles. We would have little knowledge of Paul's life and missionary journeys, and this would make it more difficult to understand his letters and theology. But is Acts historically reliable?

    a. Ancient historical standards were certainly not as uniformly insistent on factual accuracy as those in our day, but the best ancient historians had very high standards of reporting the facts and thus differed little from modern historians.

    b. Acts compares favorably to other ancient sources. It is impressively accurate in three areas: knowledge of first-century society, politics, and geography; reporting of events recorded by other ancient historians; and depictions of the history and theology of Paul.

    c. The fact that they are all presented in Luke's own style does not render the speeches of Acts untrustworthy. Luke has not given us verbatim reports but has paraphrased in his own words. This makes sense since many of the speeches were originally in Aramaic, thus requiring Luke to translate them. Further, almost all the speeches Luke reports were much longer than the summaries he has given us. Paraphrases and summaries of speeches can still accurately convey their contents, not unlike how news stories may be reported today.

2. The word of God

    a. Fulfillment. Luke carefully links the apostles' proclamation of the word of God with the word that Jesus both taught and fulfilled. The "word of God" thus binds together Luke's two volumes, as the salvation that the angel first announced on the night of Jesus' birth on a Judean hillside (Luke 2:10–12) is finally brought to the capital of the Roman Empire. Luke thus presents "the things that have been fulfilled among us" (Luke 1:1) as a continuation of the salvation history of the OT, showing how this history reaches its culmination in Christ and flows from him through the Spirit-led apostles into a new phase: the church as the people of God. Accordingly, Luke gives Christians assurance that faith is solidly grounded in the acts of God in history and that the message we believe is the same message sent from God.

b. Power. God's word is powerful. Again and again, Luke attributes the growth and strength of the church to the dynamic activity of God's word. Preaching God's word is what the apostles do wherever they go. "Received the word of God" is another way of saying "became a Christian" (11:1). Especially striking are those places where Luke, usually in transitional summaries, claims that God's word "grew" or "spread" or "increased" (6:7; 12:24; 13:49; 19:20). For Luke, God's word is especially the message about God's gracious redemption through Jesus Christ. Spiritual transformation takes place only as Christians are faithful witnesses to God's powerful word.

3. The plan of God. The outworking of God's plan is an overarching theme for Luke-Acts. Luke's gospel announces the imminent fulfillment of God's promises to Israel (1:32–33, 54–55, 68–79) in the events of Jesus' ministry, death, and resurrection, and ultimately in the creation of the end-time people of God. Acts shows how the plan of God to bring salvation to the "ends of the earth" is fulfilled in the death of his servant-Messiah and in the church's ongoing witness. Luke announces God's plan in Acts as he does in his gospel: the note of divine necessity (Acts 1:16, 21; 3:12; 4:21; 9:16; 14:21; 17:3; 19:21; 23:11; 27:24); angelic intervention (5:19, 21; 12:7–11, 23; 27:23–24); visions (10:10–16; 16:9; 18:9; 22:17–21); and the fulfillment of Scripture (1:20; 2:16–21, 25–28, 34–35; 3:22–23; 4:11, 25–26; 7:48–49; 8:31–35; 13:33–37, 40–41, 47; 15:15–18; 17:2–3; 26:22–23; 28:25–27).

Luke is especially careful to show that two vital events are rooted in God's plan: Jesus' crucifixion (e.g., 2:23; 4:27–28; 13:27) and the inclusion of Gentiles in the people of God (e.g., 10:1–16; 13:47; 15:15–18). Both events were critical yet controversial components of the early Christians' interpretation of salvation history.

4. The presence of the future. Early Christians understood that the "last days" have dawned with the coming of Christ and the Spirit. In the OT prophets, the "last days" refers to when God would fulfill his promises by saving his people and judging their enemies. Luke clearly recognizes that a day of judgment and ultimate

salvation lies in the future (cf. 3:21; 10:42), but he is particularly concerned to show that the early Christians were living in those "last days" (e.g., 2:16–17 and the many other OT quotations).

5. Salvation

a. Already/not yet. Acts continues the theme of salvation that dominates Luke (Acts 2:21, 47b; 4:12; 5:31; 13:23, 26, 47; 16:31; 28:28). The disciples initially expected that salvation would mean the restoration of an earthly kingdom to Israel (1:6). Jesus does not clearly deny that this will be the case, but his emphasis on the witness of the apostles suggests that the saving power of God's kingdom is being realized in the forgiveness of sins offered in gospel proclamation.

b. Progression. While Luke makes clear the continuity in the message of salvation, he also reveals the progressive unfolding of new implications from that message. The earliest Christians were Jews who believed that Jesus was the promised Messiah and that the messianic age had therefore dawned. These Jewish Christians continued to worship in the temple and were apparently loyal to the law and its institutions. Only by stages did the church move away from this Jewish outlook to a more universal orientation, as God made clear that he was doing a new work in which the law would no longer play a central role and in which Gentiles would share equally with the Jews in the blessings of God. Acts portrays this progression, climaxing with Paul's statement in 28:25–29: unbelieving Israel has stubbornly refused to accept Jesus the Messiah, so God's salvation is offered to the receptive Gentiles.

6. Paul. The chief instrument through which this universalizing of the church takes place is Paul. He plays a decisive role in the foundation of a new period of salvation history. We must be careful, however, not to give Paul too prominent a place since the key character in Luke-Acts is Jesus.

7. The Holy Spirit

a. Luke parallels the role of the Holy Spirit in his gospel and Acts: the Spirit anoints Jesus at the beginning of his ministry, and the Spirit strengthens the church at the beginning of its ministry; Jesus performs signs and wonders in the power of the Spirit, and the apostles heal people in the power of the Spirit; the Spirit guides events in both Luke's gospel and Acts.

b. Acts concentrates especially on the Spirit's prophetic activity: he emboldens the early Christians for witness (e.g., 4:8, 31; 7:55; 13:9) and guides the course of the apostles' ministry (8:29, 39; 11:12; 13:2; 16:6, 7; 20:22). Key here is Peter's quotation of Joel 2:28 in Acts 2:17: "I will pour out my Spirit on all people. / Your sons and your daughters will prophesy."

c. At key points in Acts, the Spirit "comes upon" or "fills" people: those who respond to Peter's Pentecost message (2:38), the Samaritans who are converted (8:15–17), Cornelius and his household (10:44). Possession of the Spirit is one of the indicators (along with faith, repentance, and water baptism) that a person belongs to the emerging people of God of the last days (11:15–17; 15:8–9).

8. The people of God. Perhaps Luke's most fundamental purpose in Acts is to help Christians answer the question "Who are we?" Two thousand years of church history sometimes prevent us from seeing just how basic that question was for the first believers. As long as only Jews were among the faithful, others could think that this new group was just another sect of Jews with a crazy idea about who the Messiah was. But as soon as Samaritans and Gentiles began entering the picture, it was impossible to identify Christianity as a subset of Judaism. Christianity was something new — in continuity with the old, of course, but distinct from it as well. Thus, a new name had to be coined to identify this new group: "Christians," followers of Christ (11:26).

G. Questions for Review and Discussion

1. Summarize what Acts is about in a single sentence.
2. How does Acts' style of literature differ from Luke's gospel?
3. Why did Luke write Acts?
4. What would be missing from our understanding of the unfolding of the history of salvation if we did not have Acts?
5. How might Acts motivate you to evangelize unbelievers?

H. Recommended Resources

Introductory

Fernando, Ajith. *Acts*. NIVAC. Grand Rapids: Zondervan, 1998.
Stott, John. *The Message of Acts: To the Ends of the Earth*. BST. Downers Grove: InterVarsity Press, 1990.

Intermediate

Longenecker, Richard N. "Acts." Pages 663–1102 in *Luke–Acts*. Rev. ed. EBC 10. Grand Rapids: Zondervan, 2007.

Marshall, I. Howard. *The Acts of the Apostles*. TNTC. Grand Rapids: Eerdmans, 1980.

Advanced

Peterson, David. *Acts*. PNTC. Grand Rapids: Eerdmans, 2009.

chapter eight

NEW TESTAMENT LETTERS

All but six of the twenty-seven NT books are letters, comprising 35 percent of the NT text. Why letters?

1. They were a convenient way to communicate at a distance.
2. They established personal presence from a distance, enabling the apostles to pastor their distant flocks.

A. New Testament Letters in Their Greco-Roman Context

Letters became an established and popular method of communication in the Greco-Roman world. A typical letter had three parts:

1. The address and greeting were usually very short, typically taking the form, "A to B, greetings." Most NT letters expand the address and change "greetings" (*chairein*) to the similar-sounding "grace" (*charis*). Ancient letters often opened with a health-wish, perhaps paralleled by the thanksgiving or blessing in NT letters.
2. The body was the longest section, and it did not have a typical sequence. Its content was as diverse as purposes for writing.
3. The conclusion ended with greetings. NT letters usually add a doxology or benediction.

NT letters resemble ancient letters, but the similarities are of a very general nature. Ancient letters are scattered across a spectrum that ranges from careful rhetorical masterpieces designed for wide dissemination to short, simple "send money" notes. The NT letters as a whole fall somewhere in the middle of this range, with some tending more toward the literary end (e.g., Romans and Hebrews) and others more toward the common end (e.g., Philemon and 3 John).

B. The Use of Scribes

The high value of writing material and the low level of literacy meant that many ancient letters were dictated to trained scribes or secretaries. Paul, for example, dictated Romans to Tertius (Rom. 16:22). The author who dictated a letter typically added a final greeting in his own hand (see 2 Thess. 3:17; Gal. 6:11). While we have no way of knowing for sure, it seems likely that most of the NT letters were produced in this way.

The freedom that an author might give to a scribe in the choice of wording differed depending on the skill of the scribe and the nature of the relationship between the writer and the scribe. We can assume that NT authors always checked the letter over and ensured its accuracy.

C. Pseudonymity and Pseudepigraphy

Pseudonymity and pseudepigraphy denote the practice of attributing written works to someone other than the real author.

1. Pseudonymity. The works in question are falsely (*pseud-*) named (*onoma*, "name"). For example, Paul is named as the author of the 1–2 Timothy and Titus, but people who believe that those letters are pseudonymous deny that Paul actually wrote them.
2. Pseudepigraphy. The works in question are falsely (*pseud-*) attributed (*epigraphos*, "superscription"). For example, Ephesians is attributed to Paul, but people who believe that Ephesians is pseudepigraphical deny that Paul actually wrote it.

Unfortunately, a majority of contemporary scholars hold that some of the NT books are pseudonymous. A broad consensus of them label Ephesians, the Pastoral Epistles, and 2 Peter pseudepigraphical. Some would add Colossians, 2 Thessalonians, and 1 Peter.

Preliminary Observations

1. Pseudepigraphy was common in the ancient world.
2. Pseudonymity must not be confused with anonymity, in which no formal claim to authorship is made. For example, the gospels and Hebrews are anonymous.
3. Pseudonymity embraces every false claim of authorship, whether for good motive or ill, and whether advanced by the real author

or by some later historical accident. It includes, for example, pen names like Mark Twain.

4. All literary forgeries are pseudepigraphical, but not all pseude-pigrapha are literary forgeries. A literary forgery is a work written or modified with the intent to deceive. Debates over the authen-ticity of NT books are tied up with the *motives* of actual authors, since the texts are so early and so stable that the ascribed author's name is there from the beginning. Motives of pseudepigraphers may include the following:
   a. pure malice
   b. money
   c. supporting a position they know to be false
   d. supporting a position they judge to be true: This was espe-cially the case in ancient "schools" in which the founder was highly venerated. Instead of publishing works under their own names, followers would publish them in the name of their founder (e.g., Pythagoras).
   e. modesty: Perhaps this is a false humility since it is a strange modesty that thinks one's own writings are so good that they could and should be attributed to an ancient biblical hero!
   f. a deep desire to be published and widely read

Evidence outside the Bible

1. Jewish literature evinces a fairly high occurrence of pseudepi-graphical literature from about the middle of the third century B.C. to the third century A.D., much of it belonging to the style of literature called "apocalyptic" (broadly defined), such as *1 Enoch*. Pseudepigraphic letters among the Jews are extremely rare.
2. Pseudonymous Christian works began to multiply around the middle of the second century A.D. They were often associated with a great Christian leader (e.g., the *Apocalypse of Peter*).
3. All the evidence points decisively in one direction regarding what the church fathers thought: pseudonymity does *not* occur in the NT.

Evidence within the NT

Many scholars seek to establish the pseudepigraphical charac-ter of a particular document on purely *internal* grounds: anachro-nisms (e.g., a reference to a computer in a letter supposedly written in 1776), a high percentage of words or phrases not found (or used quite differently than) in the known writings of the author, forms of thought and emphasis that seem at odds with the dominant strains of the agreed writings, and more.

The evidence is "spun" by scholars in different ways and given very different weight. Two other bits of internal evidence, however, bear on the discussion:

1. The author of 2 Thessalonians is aware of forgeries made in his own name. He therefore warns his readers "not to become easily unsettled or alarmed by the teaching allegedly from us — whether by prophecy or by word of mouth or by letter" (2 Thess. 2:1–2) — and provides them with some signature or token to enable them to distinguish which letters purporting to come from him were authentic and which were not (3:17).

   a. If the author was not Paul (as many scholars think), then our pseudonymous author is in the odd position of condemning pseudonymous authors — a literary forgery that damns literary forgeries.

   b. If, on the other hand, the author was Paul, then the apostle himself makes it clear that he is aware of pseudonymity and condemns the practice (at least when people are using *his* name).

2. The early Christians appear to have had no great urge to attach names of apostles to the writings they valued. More than half of the NT consists of books that do not bear the names of their authors (the four gospels, Acts, Hebrews, 1 John; even "the elder" of 2 and 3 John is not very explicit). Apparently, the truth in the documents and the evidence that the Holy Spirit was at work in the people who wrote them carried conviction, and attaching the name of an apostle *as the author* was not judged necessary — though some looser connection to an apostle obviously helped, such as Peter's standing behind Mark's gospel. The burden is on upholders of theories of pseudonymous authorship to explain why, in discarding this strong tradition of anonymity, authors would attach not their own names but other people's names to their writings.

Some Contemporary Theories

Several theories abound regarding pseudonymity and pseudepigraphy in the New Testament letters:

1. Some scholars hold that *some NT writings are falsely named or attributed and thus deceptively hypocritical*. Those who hold this view are convinced that the NT contains many examples of literary forgeries and are unembarrassed by this conclusion. Thus, the supposedly pseudonymous author of 2 Peter was a hypocrite, clearly trying to deceive his readers into thinking that the apostle Peter wrote the letter.

2. Others insist that *no NT writings are falsely named or attributed*. These scholars similarly point out how often deception plays a role in pseudepigraphy, but recall how the church universally rejected any hint of such deception. The NT documents make concrete claims that an apostle is the author. If the documents are pseudonymous, the writers *intended* to deceive in a way that is morally reprehensible — and given the nature of the documents, this is simply not credible. For example, in Ephesians the author refers to his earlier ministry, written and oral (3:3–4), his chains, and his arrangement of the ministry of Paul's other men (e.g., Tychicus, 6:21–22). He actually exhorts his readers to pray for his needs (6:19–20) when, on the assumptions of pseudonymity, the apostle was already dead! Yet he also exhorts his readers to put off falsehood and to speak truthfully (4:25; cf. also 4:15, 24; 5:9; 6:14). Similar arguments could be made about all the ostensibly pseudepigraphical works in the NT. It would seem more sensible to take the documents at face value.

3. In recent years several *mediating positions* have been advanced.
   a. Some argue that the Holy Spirit breached the gap from ostensible author to real author and that it makes no difference who the human author was. This ignores false prophecy and overlooks that these "inspired" prophets were making *historical* claims that were either true or false.
   b. The mediating position that is perhaps most widely followed today is some form of "school" theory. Those who espouse it concur with the majority opinion that certain NT documents are pseudonymous, but they argue that no deception was involved because *within the school* of those churches or writers, everyone who needed to know understood that the writing was not really from the ostensible author. This presents more problems than it resolves.

In short, the search for parallels to justify the view that the intended readers of some NT documents would have understood them to be pseudonymous, so that no deception took place, has proved a failure. The hard evidence demands that we conclude either that some NT documents are pseudonymous and that the real authors intended to deceive their readers, or that the real authors intended to speak the truth and that pseudonymity is not attested in the NT.

D. Questions for Review and Discussion

1. How do NT letters resemble ancient letters?
2. How might a contemporary office secretary parallel an ancient scribe?
3. How do pseudonymity and pseudepigraphy differ from anonymity? Give modern-day examples.
4. Do you think that pseudonymity occurs in the NT? Why?

E. Recommended Resources

Introductory

Carson, D. A. "Reading the Letters." Pages 1108–14 in *New Bible Commentary: 21st Century Edition*. Edited by D. A. Carson, R. T. France, J. A. Motyer, and G. J. Wenham. 4th ed. Downers Grove: InterVarsity Press, 1994.

Advanced

Longenecker, Richard. "On the Form, Function, and Authority of the New Testament Letters." Pages 101–14, 376 in *Scripture and Truth*. Edited by D. A. Carson and John D. Woodbridge. Grand Rapids: Zondervan, 1983.

O'Brien, Peter T. *The Letter to the Ephesians*. PNTC. Grand Rapids: Eerdmans, 1999. Especially pages 37–47.

chapter nine

PAUL: APOSTLE AND THEOLOGIAN

Paul played a vital role in the church's growth and establishment primarily by interpreting and applying God's grace in Christ. His thirteen letters make up almost one-fourth of the New Testament, and he figures in nearly a third of it if one includes Acts 13–28, which is almost entirely devoted to Paul.

A. Paul's Background

Exploring Paul's background will help us understand him better and interpret his words more accurately. Paul provides a rough outline of his background scattered throughout his letters, but the basic historical details occur in Paul's speeches in Acts 22:1–21 and 26:2–23.

1. Birth. Paul was born a citizen of the city Tarsus in Asia Minor (Acts 21:39; 22:3). More importantly, he was born a citizen of Rome (Acts 22:28), a privilege enjoyed by relatively few within the Roman Empire. His Roman citizenship was an important and providential qualification for his role as missionary to the Roman Empire (cf. Acts 16:37–39; 22:23–29; 25:10–12).
2. Upbringing. When Paul states that he was "brought up in this city" (Acts 22:3), he likely means that he spent his early years in Jerusalem. As a "Hebrew of Hebrews" (Phil. 3:5; cf. 2 Cor. 11:22), both he and his parents were thoroughly Jewish and Palestinian. To the extent that Paul's background influenced his theology, that influence was primarily Jewish and Palestinian and only secondarily Greek.
3. Education. Paul was a serious and zealous member of the influential Pharisees, Judaism's "strictest sect" (Acts 26:5; cf. 22:3;

Gal. 1:14; Phil. 3:5–6). The Pharisees paid a great deal of attention to the "oral law" ("the traditions of the elders," Mark 7:3), a body of regulations designed to interpret and supplement the written, Mosaic law. Paul trained under the famous Jewish scholar Gamaliel I (Acts 22:3), and his zeal for Judaism led him to persecute the early Christian movement (e.g., Acts 22:4a; 26:9–11; Gal. 1:13; Phil. 3:6).

4. Conversion. The persecutor of Christians became the foremost preacher of Christ by a sudden confrontation with the risen Jesus on the road to Damascus (Acts 9:3–6; 22:6–11; 26:12–15; Gal. 1:15–16). The event and its implications played a foundational role in the formation of much of Paul's theology. His conversion was sudden and dramatic, and he gives no hint of having been dissatisfied with his Jewish convictions or searching for a deeper experience of God. His conversion was also a call to ministry (Acts 9:15; 22:15; 26:15–18; Gal. 1:16), particularly to preach to Gentiles (Gal. 1:16; 1 Thess. 2:4; Rom. 1:1, 5; 15:15–16).

B. Paul's Missionary Career and Its Chronology

While referring occasionally to his early life, past travels, and future plans, Paul's letters understandably do not provide us with the kind of information necessary to reconstruct a "life of Paul." After all, Paul wrote his letters to deal with specific issues, and only where it was important to those issues, or where Paul was requesting prayer for a certain situation, does he mention his own history. Traditionally, an outline of Paul's missionary career has been built on the more detailed and sequential data provided by Luke's historically reliable account in Acts, with Paul's letters fitted into that general scheme. The following table summarizes our suggestions for this chronology.

Chronology of Paul's Missionary Career

Paul's Life		The New Testament
A.D. 34–35 (or earlier)	Conversion (Acts 9:3–6; 22:6–11; 26:12–15; Gal. 1:15–16)	

Paul's Life (cont.)		The New Testament (cont.)	
35–37	Ministry in Damascus and Arabia (Acts 9:19b–25; 2 Cor. 11:32–33; Gal. 1:17)		
37	First Jerusalem visit (Acts 9:26–30; Gal. 1:18–19)		
37–45	Ministry in Tarsus and Cilicia (Gal. 1:21–24)		
45, 46, or 47	Second Jerusalem visit (famine-relief) (Acts 11:27–30; Gal. 2:1)		
46–47 or 47–48	First missionary journey (Acts 13:1–14:28)	46–48	James
48 or 49	Apostolic Council in Jerusalem (Acts 15:1–29)	48 (just before the Jerusalem Council)	Galatians
48 or 49–51	Second missionary journey (Acts 15:36–18:22; cf. 2 Cor. 11:7–9; Phil. 4:15–16; 1 Thess. 2:2; 3:1)	50 Late 50 or early 51	1 Thessalonians 2 Thessalonians
52–57	Third missionary journey (Acts 18:23–21:15; cf. 1 Cor. 16:8; 2 Cor. 2:12–13)	Early 55 56 57	1 Corinthians 2 Corinthians Romans

Paul's Life (cont.)		*The New Testament (cont.)*	
57–59	Arrest in Jerusalem and Caesarean imprisonment (Acts 21:15–26:32)	Mid 50s–early 60s (if written from Ephesus)	Philippians
59–60	Voyage to Rome (Acts 27:1–28:10)	sometime in the late 50s or the 60s	Mark
60–62	First Roman imprisonment (Acts 28:11–31)	early 60s	Philemon, Colossians, Ephesians
62–64	Ministry in the East (cf. writings by early church fathers)	62–63	1 Peter
64–65	Second Roman imprisonment and death (cf. 2 Tim 4:6–8)	Early to mid-60s	Titus, 1 Timothy, 2 Timothy
		shortly before 65	2 Peter
		mid-60s	Acts
		middle-to-late 60s	Jude, Luke
		Not long before 70	Hebrews, Matthew
		80–85	John
		Early 90s	1–3 John
		95–96	Revelation

C. Paul's Authority and the Sources for His Thought

Paul's letters demonstrate that he knew that he was a God-called apostle with full apostolic authority. It may be confusing, then, that Paul occasionally distinguishes between his and Jesus' teaching (e.g., 1 Cor. 7:6, 10, 12; 2 Cor. 11:17). Paul does not suggest, however, that his teaching carries any less authority since what he writes is "the Lord's command" (1 Cor. 14:37). Paul's distinction is between what Jesus taught during his earthly ministry and what Jesus now teaches through Paul.

There are at least six sources of Paul's teaching:

1. Revelation. Paul's gospel came "by revelation from Jesus Christ," not from "any human source" (Gal. 1:12). This "revelation" refers to Jesus' revealing the *essence* of the gospel to Paul in one life-changing moment on the Damascus road (cf. Gal. 1:15–16).

2. Other Christians. Paul "received" (1 Cor. 15:1–5) some of the *specifics* of his teaching, such as historical details, from other Christians (cf. Gal 1:18). He probably incorporated some early Christian traditions, such as Christian hymns (e.g., possibly Phil. 2:6–11).

3. The earthly Jesus. Although he only rarely mentions an event from Jesus' ministry (besides his death and resurrection) or quotes from his teaching, Paul certainly used more of the teaching of Jesus than a mere count of quotations suggests. More important, Paul's theology is compatible with Jesus' teaching.

4. Old Testament. Paul's letters clearly quote the OT over ninety times and allude to it many more. The OT shaped Paul's thinking, and Jesus' fulfillment of the OT was the lens through which Paul read it.

5. The Greek world. Paul knew the Greek world well, and he used the Greek language and concepts to express and illuminate the gospel.

6. Judaism. Paul's own thought world was decisively formed by his Jewish upbringing. He described himself as a "Hebrew of the Hebrews" and a zealous Pharisee. He learned the OT in the context of the Judaism of his day, but his conversion forced him to reevaluate his beliefs. The complexity and significance of Paul's debt to his Jewish background is what the "new perspective" debate is about.

D. The "New Perspective" on Paul and Judaism

First-century Judaism played a critical role in the development of Paul's theology, both in his upbringing and in his interaction with various Jewish and Jewish-Christian viewpoints. This interaction is most obvious in Galatians and Romans, but it is present in varying degrees in all the letters. Determining just what the Judaism of Paul's day looked like is therefore quite significant for accurately interpreting Paul's letters.

What Is the "New Perspective"?

An extremely simplified historical sketch is necessary to set the scene for the modern debate on the "new perspective." The Protestant Reformers of the sixteenth century, especially Martin Luther and John Calvin, decisively influenced how people have traditionally understood Paul's Judaism. While reacting to certain legalistic elements in the salvation teaching of the Roman Catholic Church of their day, they tended to find the same kind of legalism in the Judaism that Paul opposed in letters like Galatians. They believed that the Jews of Paul's day held to a form of "works-righteousness": a person gained right standing with God by performing "the works of the law," meritorious deeds of obedience to the law that compelled God's favor and blessing. Against this legalism, Paul proclaimed that justification before God could be attained only by faith in the completed work of Christ, a faith that excluded any meritorious deeds. The Reformers took on the mantle of Paul, proclaiming that justification is *sola fide* (by faith alone) and *sola gratia* (by grace alone).

Most scholars embraced the Reformers' view of Judaism until E. P. Sanders challenged it in 1977 with his groundbreaking *Paul and Palestinian Judaism*. Sanders argues that Judaism was not characterized by legalism but by "covenantal nomism," that is, the covenant based on law (*nomos*). The basis for the Jews' salvation was that God chose them and entered into a covenant with them. They did not have to obey the law to be saved; they were already saved. They obeyed the law, rather, to maintain their covenantal status. Jews did not obey the law to "get in" (legalism) but to "stay in" ("nomism").

What does this new view of Judaism have to do with Paul? Sanders argues that Paul rejected covenantal nomism because he believed that salvation was found in Christ alone, not through the law and its underlying covenant. Most scholars, even those who agreed with Sanders' portrayal of first-century Judaism, were not satisfied with this response. The most satisfying and popular suggestion came from James D. G. Dunn, followed up by a host of scholars including N. T. Wright.

Dunn, who coined the phrase "new perspective," claims that what Paul opposes is the tendency of the Jews to confine salvation to their own nation and to exclude Gentiles. Paul opposes Judaism's ethnic exclusivism, not personal legalism.

The difference between Dunn's view and the traditional interpretation of Paul can perhaps be seen most clearly in their conflicting interpretations of texts such as Romans 3:20: "no human being will be justified in his [God's] sight by works of the law" (RSV; cf. also Rom. 3:28; Gal. 2:16; 3:2, 5, 10). To the Reformers, Romans 3:20 attacks Jewish works-righteousness: a person was justified by doing "works." To Dunn, Romans 3:20 attacks Jewish ethnic exclusivism: a person was justified by maintaining his covenant status by faithfully observing the Jewish law, including distinctive practices such as circumcision, Sabbath, and food laws.

Dunn and those in his wake offer a new way of reading Paul. In general, three tendencies mark the "new perspective on Paul."

1. Paul's theology is read against the background of the "story" of salvation history. (N. T. Wright is a prominent example.) The effect is to take many of the theological categories in Paul's letters that have traditionally been interpreted in terms of individual experience and restrict them to the corporate experience of Israel and the people of God.
2. The Reformers' foundational contrast between "faith" and "works" as two opposed means of being saved is reduced or even eliminated. Paul's central contrast is not with how a person gets saved but how Gentiles in the new era of salvation can be added to the people of God.
3. Paul's teaching on justification is shifted from a vertical focus (a human before God) to more of a horizontal one (Gentiles as equal partners with Jews within God's people).

In these ways, the "new perspective" tends to offer a serious and potentially damaging challenge to a hallmark of Reformation theology: justification before God by faith alone, by grace alone.

Response to the New Perspective

The new perspective on Paul has made some important contributions, correcting a skewed view of Judaism in traditional scholarship. Jews in Paul's day were certainly less legalistic than many traditional portrayals have suggested. Sanders rightly highlighted the importance of the covenant as a foundation for Jewish life and thought. Jews thought of themselves as a special people because God had chosen them by grace. Many Jews undoubtedly viewed their obedience to the law within this covenant context. They did not claim any special merit for their obedience and saw it, as Sanders has insisted, as a means of maintaining their status within God's people. The general tendency of the new perspective as a whole to redirect our attention to the Jewish matrix of Paul's thought and teaching is a welcome one. Traditional studies of Paul have sometimes focused almost exclusively on how a person gets saved and neglected how Gentiles in the new era of salvation are added to the people of God.

Nevertheless, Sanders' interpretation of Judaism and the "new perspective" is an over-reaction in the other direction. His "covenantal nomism" requires qualification:

1. Covenantal nomism was not the only understanding of salvation within first-century Judaism. Sanders' methodology is deeply flawed. Further, even if all the existing theological sources taught covenant nomism, one might still find significant pockets of legalism among the "Jews on the street." Any faith that emphasizes obedience, as Judaism undoubtedly did, is likely to produce some adherents who, perhaps through misunderstanding or lack of education, turn their obedience into a meritorious service that they think God must reward. Christianity, with considerably less emphasis on law, certainly produces such adherents. Is it not likely that, as the NT suggests, first-century Judaism did also?

2. Sanders and those who have followed him wrongly base their interpretation of first-century Judaism on the assumption that God's covenant with Israel was the starting point for Jewish obedience to the law. Many Jewish sectarian groups flourished at this time, and for some of them "getting in" was not simply a matter of God's grace revealed in the covenant, but included human works.

3. In practice for first-century Jews, salvation was through both grace and works, and it is just this combination that Paul seems to be attacking in a number of passages.

Ultimately, the new perspective, as a comprehensive explanation of Paul's relationship to Judaism, must be rejected on the basis of the single most important issue: it does not offer a better interpretation of the key texts than competing schools of thought.

1. While the Reformers may have missed some of the nuances and implications of Paul's argument regarding how Gentiles in the new era of salvation are added to the people of God, they were right to discern in Paul a key antithesis between faith and works as the means of accessing God's salvation.
2. The attempt to redefine justification in terms of covenant identity and entrance into the people of God reverses what is primary and what is secondary. Justification language refers primarily to a person's right relationship with God (vertical). A secondary consequence of justification is that the person enters the people of God (horizontal).

E. Questions for Review and Discussion

1. How does understanding Paul's context help you better understand his letters? Give a specific example.
2. What is the value of thinking through the chronology of Paul's missionary career?
3. Do you think that some of the sources of Paul's teaching are more significant than the others? Why?
4. In your own words, explain what the "new perspective on Paul" is and how you think we should respond to it.

F. Recommended Resources

Introductory

Polhill, John B. *Paul and His Letters*. Nashville: Broadman & Holman, 1999.

Intermediate

Bruce, F. F. *Paul: Apostle of the Heart Set Free*. Grand Rapids: Eerdmans, 1977.

Advanced

Schreiner, Thomas R. *Interpreting the Pauline Epistles*. Edited by Scot McKnight. Guides to New Testament Exegesis 5. Grand Rapids: Baker, 1990.

———. *Paul, Apostle of God's Glory in Christ: A Pauline Theology*. Downers Grove: InterVarsity Press, 2001.

Thielman, Frank. *Theology of the New Testament: A Canonical and Synthetic Approach*. Grand Rapids: Zondervan, 2005. Pages 219–479.

Westerholm, Stephen. *Perspectives Old and New on Paul: The "Lutheran" Paul and His Critics*. Grand Rapids: Eerdmans, 2004.

chapter ten

ROMANS

A. What Is Romans About?

Romans is Paul's longest letter and includes his most significant teachings.

1. The introduction (1:1–17) concludes with a transition that states the letter's theme: the gospel is the revelation of God's righteousness, which people can experience only by faith (1:16–17).

2. The gospel is the righteousness of God by faith (1:18–4:25). Sin has gained a stranglehold on all people that only an act of God—experienced as a gift received through faith—can break (1:18–3:20). The way to become innocent before God is through the sacrifice of his Son (3:21–26). This justification can be gained only by faith (3:27–31), as the story of Abraham clearly illustrates (4:1–25).

3. The gospel is the power of God for salvation in both our present earthly life and future judgment (5:1–8:39). Being justified results in peace with God and a secure hope for vindication on judgment day (5:1–11). The ground for this hope is the believer's relationship to Christ, who reversed the effects of Adam's sin (5:12–21). Christians must confidently battle the powers of this present realm: sin (6:1–23), the law (7:1–25), and death and the flesh (8:1–13). The Spirit assures Christians that they are God's children and will experience glorification (8:14–39).

4. The relationship between the gospel and Israel raises a question that requires vindicating God's righteousness (9:1–11:36): Does transferring covenant privileges from Israel to the church mean that God has spurned his promises to Israel? We are assured that that is certainly not the case (9:1–6a):

       a. God's promises were never intended to guarantee salvation to every Israelite by birth (9:6b–29).

       b. Israelites failed to embrace God's righteousness in Christ (9:30–10:21).

       c. Some Israelites, like Paul, are being saved (11:1–10).

       d. It is only through Israel that salvation has come to Gentiles, and God's promise to Israel will come to full realization when "all Israel will be saved" (11:11–36).

5. The gospel transforms lives (12:1–15:13). God's grace should stimulate many forms of sacrificial service permeated by love (12:1–21). Christians may not ignore government's legitimate claims or the summarizing commandment to love their neighbors as themselves (13:1–14). Stronger and weaker Christians must respect and tolerate each other's views on observing certain dietary codes and rituals (14:1–15:13).

6. The conclusion presents Paul's situation and travel plans, greetings to Roman Christians, a warning about false teachers, personal notes, and a benediction (15:14–16:27).

B. Who Wrote Romans?

Romans claims to have been written by Paul (1:1), and there has been no serious challenge to this claim. Tertius was probably Paul's scribe (16:22).

C. Where Was Romans Written?

Paul plans to travel to three places: Jerusalem, Rome, and Spain (15:22–29). He hopes to give Jewish Christians in Jerusalem an offering from the Gentile-Christian churches he has planted (15:25–27, 30–33), and he views his trip to Rome as a stopping-off point on his way to Spain (15:24, 28; cf. 15:19–20). Since Paul must be near the end of his third missionary journey as he writes Romans (Acts 19:21; 20:16), Corinth is the most likely place of writing (Acts 20:3 and 2 Cor. 13:1, 10; cf. Rom. 16:1–2, 23 and 1 Cor. 1:14).

D. When Was Romans Written?

When Paul wrote Romans depends on the date of Paul's three-month stay in Greece, which depends on the chronology of Paul's life and ministry. The best option is about A.D. 57 (see the table in ch. 9).

E. To Whom Was Romans Written?

Paul addresses the letter to "all in Rome who are loved by God and called to be saints" (NIV 1:7; cf. 1:15). We have no definite evidence concerning the origin of the church in Rome or its structure at the time Paul wrote to it. The most likely scenario is that Jews who were converted on the Day of Pentecost (Acts 2:10) were the first to bring the gospel there. When Rome temporarily expelled Jewish Christians, those Gentiles who had been attracted to Christianity would have taken over the church. When Jewish Christians later returned, they would probably be in a minority and perhaps viewed with some condescension by the now-dominant Gentile wing.

There are at least three options for Paul's audience:

1. Entirely or mainly Jewish Christians
2. Entirely or mainly Gentile Christians
3. Both Jewish and Gentile Christians

Although the second option is more likely than the first (cf. 1:5–6), the third option is most likely (1:7). While Paul's audience certainly includes Gentiles (1:13; 11:13), it presumably includes the Jewish Christians he greets in chapter 16 as well, and the "weak in faith" (14:1–15:13) are quite possibly a Jewish-Christian faction.

F. Why Was Romans Written?

What was Paul's purpose in sending such a heavy theological letter to Roman Christians? The letter does not explicitly state its purpose, and the only remaining method of determining its purpose is to fit its contents to its particular occasion. Opinions on Paul's motivations in writing tend to emphasize the circumstances of either Paul or the Christian community in Rome.

The Situation of Paul

Views that single out Paul's own circumstances as decisive may be divided according to the places central to Paul's concerns.

1. Spain. According to some scholars, Paul's primary reason for writing this letter is to establish a relationship with the Roman Christians so that they would financially support his mission to plant new churches in Spain (15:24–29). Had this been Paul's overriding purpose, however, we would have expected mention of Spain long before chapter 15. Nor does this adequately explain Paul's select

treatment of theological topics from a perspective that traces the history of salvation regarding the law and gospel, Jew and Greek.

2. Galatia/Corinth. Other scholars would say that Paul's chief reason for writing this letter is to share his mature views on Jewish issues, which he dealt with in his struggle with Judaizers in Galatia and Corinth. This view, while partially right, leaves one crucial question unanswered: Why send this theological dissertation to Rome?

3. Jerusalem. Still others believe that Paul's principal reason for writing this letter is to "rehearse" the speech he anticipates giving in Jerusalem when he arrives there with the collection (see 15:30–33). The objections to the previous two views both apply here: (1) it leaves the purpose of the letter separate from Paul's desire to visit Rome (which Paul emphasizes in both the introduction and conclusion), and (2) it does not explain why Paul sends this theological treatise to Rome.

The Situation of the Roman Christians

Other views emphasize the circumstances of the Roman Christians, particularly the one passage in Romans in which it appears that Paul has a specific problem in mind (14:1–15:13). This section rebukes two groups for their intolerance toward each other: the "weak in faith" (probably mainly Jewish Christians) and the "strong in faith" (probably mainly Gentile Christians). The rebuke focuses on the Gentile Christians, who are becoming arrogant toward the shrinking minority of Jewish Christians. This text, it is argued, is the center of Romans.

Although one of Paul's purposes in writing this letter was to heal this division in the Christian community in Rome, we doubt that this was his primary purpose.

1. It is hard to understand why Paul would have waited until chapter 14 to make a practical application of this theology.

2. The content of chapters 1–11 does not serve as a basis for the exhortations in 14:1–15:13.

3. Paul does not necessarily address the specific needs of the Roman church exactly as he does in other letters.

Several Purposes

Paul's purpose in Romans cannot be confined to any of these specific suggestions. It may be better to speak of Paul's *several* purposes in Romans. A number of intersecting factors come together to form what we might call Paul's missionary situation, and it is out of that situation that he writes to the Romans. Multiple circumstances lead Paul to write a letter in which he carefully sets forth his understanding of the gospel, particularly as it relates to salvation and the historical question of Jew and Gentile, law and gospel, and continuity and discontinuity between the old and the new:

1. Past battles in Galatia and Corinth
2. The coming crisis in Jerusalem
3. The need to secure a missionary base for the work in Spain
4. The importance of unifying the divided Christian community in Rome around the gospel
5. Misguided attacks against his theology as being anti-law and perhaps anti-Jewish (see 3:8)

G. What Style of Literature Is Romans?

Although Romans is often viewed as a timeless treatise for every generation of Christians, its message is embedded in a document written to a particular audience in a definite situation (1:1–17; 15:14–16:27). To put it simply, Romans is a letter.

But what kind of letter? There were many types of letters in the ancient world, ranging from brief requests for money from children away from home to long essays intended to reach a wide audience (see ch. 8). Paul's letters generally fall somewhere between these extremes, but Romans is farther toward the latter end of the spectrum than any other of his letters (with the possible exception of Ephesians). Romans is a treatise that formally and systematically unpacks a theological argument, which Paul develops according to the inner logic of the gospel. Not once in chapters 1–13 does Paul allude to a specific circumstance or individual within the Roman Christian community.

H. What Does Romans Contribute to Our Understanding of the Faith?

It is possible that Romans does not have a single theme, but rather has recurring motifs within several distinct topics. If we are to single out one theme, however, a good case can be made for "the gospel."

1. Gospel. Opinions vary about the "central" theme of Romans. The focus has tended over time to move from the beginning to the end of the letter: justification by faith (chs. 1–4), union with

Christ and the work of God's Spirit (chs. 6–8), the history of salvation and of Jews and Gentiles within this history (chs. 9–11), and practical exhortation to unity (14:1–15:13). Each of these four positions is alive in current scholarship, though sometimes in modified form.

    a. This word and its related verb "to evangelize" are prominent in the introduction and conclusion, where we might expect to encounter any overarching topic.

    b. "Gospel" is foremost in 1:16–17, which is often (and probably rightly) taken to be the statement of the letter's theme.

    c. Romans grows out of Paul's missionary situation, which would make a focus on the gospel quite natural.

2. Theological focus. Although Romans is not a timeless summary of Paul's theology, it is much less tied to specific first-century circumstances than almost any other book of the NT. Its unfolding of the gospel is systematic and accessible for readers today.

3. Continuity and discontinuity. Romans addresses the most important issue that the early church had to face: the degree of continuity and discontinuity between Israel and the church. Romans supplies the basic building blocks for the foundation of a *Christian* theology.

4. Individual salvation. Paul's gospel has important implications for the relation of Jews and Gentiles, but Romans 1–8 makes clear that Paul's gospel targets individual human beings, locked up under sin and in need of the redemption available only in Jesus Christ.

5. Justification. Justification by faith is a critical component of Paul's presentation of the gospel. To be "justified" is to be declared right with God. This verdict, Paul insists in Romans, is a manifestation of pure grace on God's part and therefore can be attained by sinful human beings only through faith. The contemporary theological climate challenges this Reformation understanding of "justification by faith" at a number of points, but a careful reading of Romans reaffirms its truth and reminds us of its critical importance for the power of the gospel.

6. Practical application. Romans is the greatest work of theology ever written, so it is understandable that the tendency when explaining its significance is to dwell on its theology. But Romans insists that the gospel is both thoroughly theological *and* practical. As the phrase "the obedience of faith" suggests at the beginning of the letter (1:5 NRSV; cf. 16:26), the gospel

Paul presents in Romans is a life-transforming message. Faith in Christ must always be accompanied by obedience to him as Lord. Chapters 12–16 are not an afterthought or appendix to Romans; they are present precisely because the gospel is not truly understood or responded to unless it has changed the people it addresses. The lordship of Christ and the indwelling of the Spirit must inevitably change the way we "think" (12:2) and, thus, ultimately, the way we live.

I. Questions for Review and Discussion

1. How is the literary style of Romans different from most of Paul's other letters? How does that affect how you read Romans?
2. What are Paul's purposes for writing Romans? Why is it helpful to be aware of these purposes?
3. What are some major themes that people have suggested for Romans? What do you think is the central theme?
4. If Romans 1–11 is primarily theology, then the rest of the letter is primarily application. What is the relation between theology and application? Should one be valued more than the other? Is one expendable?
5. What specific passage in Romans is especially precious to you? How does that passage relate to the letter as a whole?

J. Recommended Resources

Introductory

Edwards, James R. *Romans.* NIBC. Peabody: Hendrickson, 1992.

Moo, Douglas J. *Encountering the Book of Romans: A Theological Survey.* Grand Rapids: Baker, 2002.

Stott, John. *Romans: God's Good News for the World.* BST. Downers Grove: InterVarsity Press, 1994.

Intermediate

Moo, Douglas J. *Romans.* NIVAC. Grand Rapids: Zondervan, 2000.

Advanced

Moo, Douglas J. *The Epistle to the Romans.* NICNT. Grand Rapids: Zondervan, 1996.

Westerholm, Stephen. *Understanding Paul: The Early Christian Worldview of the Letter to the Romans.* Grand Rapids: Baker, 2004.

chapter eleven

1 AND 2 CORINTHIANS

The Corinthian letters are less formal and systematic than Romans. They are "occasional" letters since they address specific people and are occasioned by concrete issues.

A. What Are 1 and 2 Corinthians About?

1 Corinthians

1. Paul opens with a greeting and thanksgiving (1:1–9).
2. The church divisively views Christian leaders (1:10–4:21). They identify themselves with particular leaders for their wisdom and eloquence (1:10–17), but the cross of Christ reveals God's wisdom (1:18–2:5). So does the Spirit, who enables individuals to understand it (2:6–16). But the Corinthian believers arrogantly and foolishly esteem their leaders with childish divisiveness, not realizing that leaders are merely God's farmhands, construction workers, and stewards who are accountable for the quality of their work (3:1–4:7). They should imitate Paul, who cautions them and advises them of an impending visit (4:8–21).
3. In response to reports, Paul addresses three problems: a case of incest (5:1–13), lawsuits between believers (6:1–11), and sexual immorality (6:12–20).
4. In response to a written inquiry from the Corinthians (7:1), Paul addresses six significant topics that were raised:
   a. Marriage and related matters (7:1–40)
   b. Food sacrificed to idols (8:1–11:1). Self-sacrificial love must resolve controversies over eating food that has been sacrificed to idols (8:1–11; 10:23–11:1). Paul voluntarily lays aside his "rights" as an apostle in order to win as many as possible to Christ (9:1–23) and exhorts his fellow Chris-

tians to imitate his self-discipline (9:24–27). The history of Israel illustrates an unfortunate tendency to begin well, not persevere, and consequently incur God's judgment (10:1–13). Christians must flee idolatry by not participating in pagan temple worship (10:14–22).

c. The relationship between men and women, especially regarding head coverings for women when the church gathered (11:2–16)

d. Abuses at the Lord's Supper (11:17–34)

e. The distribution and exercise of the Spirit's gifts (12:1–14:40). The church needs diversity in unity (12:1–31), love (13:1–13), and intelligibility and proper order in its public meetings (14:1–40). Paul emphasizes the relative value of prophecy and tongues (14:1–25).

f. The resurrection of believers (15:1–58): The proper prototype is Jesus' bodily resurrection.

5. Paul concludes with instructions about a special collection, personal requests, exhortations, and greetings (16:1–24).

2 Corinthians

1. Paul opens with a greeting and lengthy, emotional thanksgiving (1:1–11).

2. Paul defends his travel plans (1:12–2:13).

3. The nature of Christian ministry is tied to a proper estimate of end-time tensions, namely, the last days have already begun, but they are not yet consummated (2:14–7:4). God himself has made Paul competent for this new covenant ministry (2:14–3:6), which is superior to ministry under the old covenant (3:7–18). Paul is committed to proclaim the gospel with integrity (4:1–6). Jesus is the treasure, and Paul and his ministry are mere jars of clay that carry around the treasure (4:7–15). His future eternal glory far outweighs any troubles (4:16–5:10), and the love of Christ compels him to proclaim reconciliation as Christ's ambassador (5:11–21). Paul pleads with the Corinthians to open their hearts to his ministry and flee idolatry (6:1–7:4).

4. Paul is almost euphoric with relief that the Corinthians have responded with repentance and godly sorrow to his earlier rebukes by visit and letter (7:5–16). This allows him to exhort them to give generously to the collection for the Christians in Jerusalem (8:1–9:15).

5. Paul responds to a fresh outbreak of opposition at Corinth (10:1 – 13:10). He appeals for obedient faith (10:1 – 6) and condemns the opposition for its ugly boasting (10:7 – 18). He exposes false apostles (11:1 – 15) and answers fools according to their folly, engaging in a little boasting of his own by inverting all the criteria of his opponents and boasting in things they would despise (11:16 – 12:10). Paul chides the Corinthians for not taking decisive action against the opponents, who are channeling the church toward a cross-disowning triumphalism; he assures them that he is not trying to burden or exploit them (12:11 – 21). He begs the Corinthian believers to reconsider their course and warns them that if necessary, he will take strong action when he arrives on his third visit (13:1 – 10).

6. Paul concludes with a final appeal, greetings, and benediction (13:11 – 14).

B. Who Wrote 1 and 2 Corinthians?

Paul is identified as the author in the opening verses of both letters, and few have contested the claim.

C. When Were 1 and 2 Corinthians Written?

There is one fixed point. In Acts 18:12-17, we read that "while Gallio was proconsul of Achaia," the Corinthian Jews made an attack on Paul. Based on an inscription with an announcement by the Emperor Claudius, we know that Gallio held this office for one year beginning July 1, A.D. 51 (or less likely, 52). After Gallio dismissed the Jews' case against Paul, Paul "stayed on in Corinth for some time" (Acts 18:18) and then "sailed for Syria," probably in the spring of 52. After spending some time in Palestine, he embarked on his next missionary journey, coming quickly to Ephesus. Paul's two-and-a-half-year stint in Ephesus would have taken him to the spring of 55. Paul wrote 1 Corinthians while he was in Ephesus, probably early in 55, and completed 2 Corinthians within the next year or so while he was in Macedonia (2 Cor. 2:12 – 13; 7:5; 8:1 – 5; 9:2).

D. To Whom and Why Were 1 and 2 Corinthians Written?

What Was Corinth Like?

Corinth, a Roman colony, was located on the isthmus that connects the Peloponnese with the rest of Greece. It was a port city ideally situated for commerce, populated by Romans, Greeks, and Jews, freedmen and slaves, rich and poor. Romans dominated the scene with their laws, culture, and religion.

It is unfair to read the old city's character into the new city. For example, in the old Corinth (prior to becoming a Roman colony), "to Corinthianize" meant "to commit sexual immorality," and "Corinthian girl" referred to a prostitute. The new Corinth did not necessarily continue such associations, although it is unlikely that it was known for its moral purity (cf. 1 Cor. 6:12–20).

What Social Influences Helped to Shape the Corinthians' Worldview?

The immature Christians at Corinth were affected by a number of social pressures:

1. The city's own pagan past was the most likely source of the erroneous Corinthian approach to wisdom and spirituality.
2. Corinth was a city where one could make a fortune and then rise in power, wealth, and honor. The corrupt Roman patronage system provided a way to scramble up the social ladder. Powerful patrons provided their clients with money, contacts, and inclusion; the recipients, in return, promoted the reputations of their benefactors. It was an endless cycle of carefully calibrated self-promotion.
3. The Greek and the Roman worlds so emphasized rhetoric that gifted speakers were admired and followed like movie stars are today. Lecturing was both an art form and a critical component of public and political communication.

The Corinthians' problem was not a relapse into paganism; rather, their Christian faith, however sincere, had not yet transformed the worldview they had inherited from the surrounding culture. Moreover, their knowledge of the gospel did not keep them from arrogantly destroying weaker Christians (8:1–11:1) and divisively elevating certain charismatic gifts above love (12–14). It was easy for a people not gripped by the functional centrality of the gospel to become infatuated with those who were skilled in rhetoric; hence, the Corinthians had become slightly contemptuous of Paul's commitment to preach Christ crucified rather than impress people with eloquence (1 Cor. 2:1–5; 2 Cor. 10:10; 11:5-6).

The problems of factionalism and immature expectations recur in 2 Corinthians, where Paul still finds himself having to explain the theology of the cross: God's grace is perfected in weakness. Further, the Corinthians' stress on their own maturity reflects an overconfidence that neither understands nor anticipates the blessings still to come.

Who Were Paul's Opponents in 1 and 2 Corinthians?

There are so many theories as to the nature of Paul's opponents in these two letters that we should supplement our earlier historical reconstruction by noting three caveats:

1. There is no evidence that at the time of writing 1 Corinthians Paul was facing a church that had been taken over by leaders *from the outside.* By the time of 2 Corinthians 10–13, that had certainly happened. Thus, one must not read the situation of 2 Corinthians back into 1 Corinthians.
2. There is no evidence that the root cause of the opposition behind 1 Corinthians was the influence of Judaizers, Jews who in some sense accept Jesus as the Messiah but who insist that Gentiles convert to Judaism before (or at least as part of) coming to faith in Jesus.
3. There is no evidence that the dominant problem confronting Paul was full-blown Gnosticism (see ch. 23).

We can, however, describe Paul's opponents in three ways:

1. They are simultaneously divided against each other and, in some measure, opposed to Paul.
2. They arrogantly assume that all or most of the blessings of the age to come are already being experienced to their fullest extent. This view of spirituality deprecates the material and has more to do with status than ethics.
3. The opponents in 2 Corinthians 10–13 were a new kind of Judaizers. They seem to be less concerned with circumcision and detailed observance of the Mosaic law than with prestige and power in accordance with the contemporary values of Corinthian society.

E. How Do the Historical Puzzle Pieces Fit Together?

Paul first preached the gospel in Corinth for about a year and a half during his second missionary journey (Acts 18). He subsequently wrote the Corinthians at least four letters, two of which have not survived:

1. Corinthians A: This letter forbade association with immoral people (1 Cor. 5:9).
2. Corinthians B (1 Corinthians): About one year after Paul's initial ministry in Corinth, he ministered fruitfully in Ephesus for two and a half years, during which he wrote 1 Corinthians. Meanwhile, others had come to build on the foundation that Paul had laid in Corinth, and the spiritually immature Corinthians formed partisan groups around various leaders (1 Cor. 1:11–12). Their integrity was marred by the issues Paul responds to in chapters 5–15 (see above).
3. Corinthians C: The situation at Corinth was not improving, so Paul changed his travel plans (1 Cor. 16:5–8; 2 Cor. 1:15–16). The church had been invaded by some self-designated Christian leaders whom Paul dubs "false apostles" (2 Cor. 11:13–15). Paul's visit to Corinth turned into a distressing confrontation, which Paul had warned about (1 Cor. 4:21) and later called a "painful visit" (2 Cor. 2:1). From Paul's perspective at the time, this visit was a complete fiasco. He resolved not to return immediately to spare another painful confrontation, but he was charged with being fickle (1:16–2:4). To clarify his expectations, he wrote a third letter (Corinthians C), sometimes called the "tearful letter" or "severe letter" because he wrote them "out of great distress and anguish of heart and with many tears" (2:4) and demanded that the malicious ringleader be punished (see 2:3–9; 7:8–12).
4. Corinthians D (2 Corinthians): Paul did not know how his severe letter had been received, and when Titus arrived and shared the news, Paul's distress rapidly changed to elation (2 Cor. 7:6–10). His response in 2 Corinthians 1–9 breathes a sigh of relief that the worst is over. That is what makes 2 Corinthians 10–13 so difficult to interpret: the tone in these chapters assumes that the situation in Corinth had become desperately dangerous yet again (see below).

F. What About 2 Corinthians 10–13?

The historical and social reconstructions described above are based on solid evidence, which supports the premise that 1 Corinthians and 2 Corinthians 1–9 are genuine units, not a patchwork of letter fragments. The place of 2 Corinthians 10–13, however, is widely disputed because its tone is so different from chapters 1–9. Are chapters

1–9 and 10–13 sufficiently different enough in tone to throw doubt on the assumption that they were written at the same time, under the same circumstances, in one letter? Four principal theories address this issue:

1. Second Corinthians 10–13 is the painful and severe letter (Corinthians C), and 2 Corinthians 1–9 is Corinthians D. The advantage of this theory is that it fully explains the remarkable difference in tone between chapters 1–9 (joyful and confident) and 10–13 (angry, broken, and scathingly ironic). This theory, however, introduces more problems than it solves. For example, chapters 10–13 do not include the one thing we are certain must have been in the severe letter: the demand that a certain offender be punished (2:5–6; 7:12). Also, no Greek manuscript of 2 Corinthians suggests that the epistle originally terminated at the end of chapter 9 or that chapters 10–13 had an introduction typical of Paul's letters.

2. Second Corinthians 1–13 was written at one time. This coheres with the textual evidence, and there is no shortage of theories for explaining the remarkable change in tone between chapters 1–9 and 10–13. In our judgment, however, the differences in tone and emphasis are sufficiently strong that some account must be given of them, and the proposed solutions are not very satisfying.

3. Second Corinthians 10–13 is a fifth letter (Corinthians E), following 2 Corinthians 1–9 (Corinthians D). This is the most popular theory among recent commentators. The primary advantage of this explanation is that it fully accounts for the profound difference in tone between chapters 1–9 and 10–13. This theory is possible (and better than the first two), but it must rely rather heavily on the existence of a stupid scribe early in the manuscript tradition.

4. Second Corinthians 10–13 was written a bit after 2 Corinthians 1–9 but as part of the same letter. This minor modification to the third theory improves it. Paul was eager to hear from Titus (2 Cor. 2:13), so it is natural to assume that, once he heard Titus' good report, he immediately set about communicating his relief to the Corinthians. He was grateful that his severe letter (Corinthians C) had not done the damage he feared, delighted that the Corinthians had responded with repentance and obedience, and encouraged to learn that his most dangerous opponent had been

disciplined. But there is no reason to think that he finished his long letter promptly. He was at this same time extraordinarily pressed by his ministry in Macedonia, and it is not unreasonable to suppose that the completion of the letter was delayed for weeks, or even longer. If during that time Paul received additional information about the situation in Corinth and learned that the church had once again plummeted into a disastrous state, the abrupt change of tone that begins at 10:1 would be justified. It seems reasonable to postulate that Paul received bad news from Corinth after finishing chapters 1–9 but before completing the letter and sending it off, and thus changed his tack in chapters 10–13.

There is not sufficient evidence to give a decisive account of 2 Corinthians 10–13, but the fourth theory seems marginally stronger than the third, which is in turn considerably more believable than either the first or the second.

G. What Do 1 and 2 Corinthians Contribute to Our Understanding of the Faith?

1. Gospel application. These letters show how the unchanging gospel, taught in the languages and cultures of the first century, was first applied to changing circumstances. For instance, the particular form of the Corinthian denial of the resurrection may not be popular in the twentieth century, but Paul's strenuous insistence on the historical reality of the resurrection of Jesus as a nonnegotiable part of the gospel may be applied in many circumstances (1 Cor. 15).
2. Law. They contribute to the debate over Paul's view of the law. Paul imposes some restraints (1 Cor. 9:19–23), where in other passages he seems to see himself as free from law.
3. Relationships between men and women. They contribute to an understanding of manhood and womanhood (1 Cor. 11:2–16; 14:34–35).
4. Spiritual gifts. They contribute to the nature of prophecy, the place of the "grace-gifts," and the theology of the Spirit (1 Cor. 12–14).
5. Resurrection. They contain not only the earliest written list of the witnesses of Jesus' resurrection but the most important NT treatment of the nature of the resurrection (1 Cor. 15).

6. Paul. They most clearly illuminate the character of Paul the man, Christian, pastor, and apostle. This provides substance for Paul's invitation to imitate him and thereby imitate Christ (1 Cor. 11:1).

7. Church. They make an enormous contribution to our understanding of the church: its nature, unity, diversity, characteristics, conduct, interdependence, and discipline.

8. Pride. They strongly condemn arrogance, self-promotion, boasting, and self-confidence.

9. Cross-centered life. They passionately connect a theology of the cross with cross-centered living. Paul rejects the integration of godly teaching with pagan values of self-promotion. The cross not only justifies sinners, but also teaches them how to live and die, how to lead and follow, how to love and serve. Paul emphasizes service, self-denial, purity, and weakness as the matrix in which God displays his strength. Perhaps the high-water mark is the emphasis on love as "the most excellent way" all Christians must pursue (1 Cor. 12:31–13:13).

H. Questions for Review and Discussion

1. At least how many letters did Paul write to the Corinthian church? Briefly explain the purpose of each one.

2. How does the social baggage that influences your worldview compare and contrast with that of the Corinthians?

3. What issues that Paul addresses are particularly relevant in your current church context?

I. Recommended Resources

Introductory

Blomberg, Craig L. 1 Corinthians. NIVAC. Grand Rapids: Zondervan, 1994.

Carson, D. A. From Triumphalism to Maturity: An Exposition of 2 Corinthians 10–13. Grand Rapids: Baker, 1984. Reprinted as A Model of Christian Maturity, 2007.

———. The Cross and Christian Ministry: An Exposition of Passages from 1 Corinthians. Grand Rapids: Baker, 1993. Reprinted with the subtitle Leadership Lessons from 1 Corinthians, 2004.

Hafemann, Scott J. 2 Corinthians. NIVAC. Grand Rapids: Zondervan, 2000.

Mahaney, C. J. *Living the Cross-Centered Life: Keeping the Gospel the Main Thing.* Sisters, OR: Multnomah, 2006.

Intermediate

Garland, David E. *2 Corinthians.* NAC 29. Nashville: Broadman & Holman, 2000.

Advanced

Barnett, Paul. *The Second Epistle to the Corinthians.* NICNT. Grand Rapids: Eerdmans, 1997.

Carson, D. A. *Showing the Spirit: A Theological Exposition of 1 Corinthians 12–14.* Grand Rapids: Baker, 1987.

Ciampa, Roy E., and Brian S. Rosner. *1 Corinthians.* PNTC. Grand Rapids: Eerdmans, 2010.

Fee, Gordon D. *The First Epistle to the Corinthians.* NICNT. Grand Rapids: Eerdmans, 1987.

chapter twelve

GALATIANS

A. What Is Galatians About?

1. Paul's greeting highlights his status as a God-sent apostle (1:1–5). Noticeably absent from the introduction is thanksgiving. Instead, Paul expresses astonishment that the Galatians are deserting not only the exclusive gospel but God himself (1:6–10).

2. Paul defends his status as an apostle and states the crux of the problem (1:11–2:21). The other apostles have accepted Paul's calling to the Gentiles, similar to Peter's calling to the Jews (2:6–10). Paul recounts how he rebuked Peter for withdrawing fellowship from Gentile Christians, emphasizing that even Jews are saved not by works of the law but by faith in Christ (2:11–16). The heart of the issue is Christ versus law: sinners who are justified in Christ have died to the law and live "by faith in the Son of God" (2:17–21).

3. Justification is obtained by faith alone (3:1–4:31). The Galatians received the Spirit by faith, not by obeying the law (3:1–5). Abraham illustrates this (3:6–29): he was justified by faith (3:6–9) and given a promise that in his offspring *all* the nations of the earth would be blessed. By contrast, the law of Moses curses sinners, and it is this very curse that Christ bore in their place (3:10–14). The law cannot take precedence over or replace the covenant of promise that God made with Abraham 430 years earlier; rather, the law was a temporary provision until Christ came (3:15–25). Approaching God by faith removes all human distinctions (3:26–29). Consequently, believers have reached "adulthood" and may function as sons rather than as minors still under the jurisdiction of household slaves (4:1–7).

But the Galatians are backsliding into the bondage of law from which God had rescued them, so Paul pleads again that they stop (4:8–20). Abraham's sons through Hagar and Sarah physically and spiritually illustrate the difference between living in slavery and living in freedom (4:21–31).

4. Christians are free, which has implications for how they live (5:1–6:10). They should live in the freedom that Christ has won for them and reject circumcision (5:1–12). They ought to live in the Spirit rather than in the flesh (5:13–26) and do good to all, especially other Christians (6:1–10).

5. Paul closes with an admonition about circumcision and a benediction (6:11–18).

B. Who Wrote Galatians?

Paul claims to have written this letter (1:1), and the claim rings indisputably true.

C. To Whom Was Galatians Written?

A number of Gauls migrated to Asia Minor in the third century B.C., and by the first century B.C. their kingdom stretched south to what is now Turkey. The Romans conquered this area in 25 B.C. and made it the province of Galatia. The problem for us is whether the "Galatians" to whom Paul wrote refers to (1) ethnic Galatians in the north of the province or (2) southerners of various races who were included in the Roman province. Here is a sampling of arguments in favor of North or South Galatia:

North Galatia

1. Galatia referred to the place inhabited by the Gauls in the north. (But this was also used of the whole province.)

2. "Galatia" would not be used of Phrygians and the like because it would remind them of their subjection to Rome. (But Paul referred to himself as a Roman citizen, and Galatia was the only term that covered all the cities mentioned.)

South Galatia

1. We have information about people and places Paul knew and visited in the southern region (Acts 13–14), but none at all in the north.

2. Paul "traveled throughout the region of Phrygia and Galatia" (Acts 16:6), the area through which he would go when he left Lystra (16:2).
3. "Galatians" was the only word available that embraced the people in all the cities of the first missionary journey: Antioch, Lystra, Iconium, and Derbe.

There is no final proof for either the North or South Galatian theories. The arguments in favor of the South Galatian theory, however, are considerably more compelling.

D. When Was Galatians Written?

Based on the South Galatian theory, Paul wrote Galatians in about A.D. 48; the North Galatian theory pushes the date back to the late 50s. The main issue is whether Paul is writing before or after the Jerusalem Council (Acts 15), which occurred in about 48. The most plausible view is that Paul wrote Galatians just prior to the Jerusalem Council, not least because the letter does not mention the Council's verdict. This means that Paul's two visits to Jerusalem mentioned in Galatians 1:18–24 and 2:1–10 correspond with the visits mentioned in Acts 9:26–30 and 11:25–30 (not Acts 15).

The Roman Provinces of Asia Minor

E. Why Was Galatians Written?

Paul wrote Galatians to guard the gospel because the Galatians were in danger of forsaking it. When he learned what was happening in Galatia, he immediately wrote them a passionate defense of justification by faith alone in Christ alone (2:16–17; 3:8, 11, 24). In addition to defending his authority (from 1:1 to 6:17) and motives (1:10; 2:1–5; 5:11) as an apostle, he refutes two opposing strands of false teaching:

1. Libertinism (an abuse of Christian liberty). Using Christian liberty to justify sin perverts the gospel, so Paul commands, "Do not use your freedom to indulge the sinful nature" (5:13). In every age it has been tempting to deduce that if we are saved by grace, it does not matter how we live.
2. Legalism (a rejection of Christian liberty). Justification by keeping the law also perverts the gospel. After Paul and Barnabas left South Galatia (Acts 13–14), apparently some Jewish "Christians" arrived and taught that Christians must submit to Jewish law, particularly circumcision (5:2–6; 6:12; cf. 4:9–10, 21). But a return to the Mosaic law betrayed an inability to grasp how the law properly functioned across the sweep of redemptive history.

Advocates of the "new perspective" on Paul (see ch. 9) argue that the false teachers in Galatia emphasized the law's "boundary markers" that differentiated Jews from other people: circumcision, food laws, and Sabbath. Paul, then, opposes such divisive boundary markers because he wants to build a unified church with both Jews and Gentiles. This supposition, however, is too narrow: (1) the law functions as much more than mere boundary markers (Gal. 3), and (2) the heart of Paul's argument is tied to the exclusive sufficiency of the cross of Christ to see a person declared "just" before God.

F. What Does Galatians Contribute to Our Understanding of the Faith?

This short letter has far greater importance than its size might suggest.

1. Faith vs. works. Justification comes only through faith in Christ. This is important to clarify often since (1) people tend to think that they can earn their salvation — however it is understood — and (2) many misunderstand Christianity as nothing more than a

system of morality. Whether by observing rituals or living morally, sinners cannot improve on what God has done in Christ.

2. Salvation history. Paul's appeal to Abraham (3:6–29) helps us understand the way the Bible hangs together as one book. His argument hinges on reading Scripture in its proper sequence in the unfolding history of redemption: (1) the promise to Abraham, (2) the law of Moses, and (3) fulfillment in Christ. Instead of assuming that Abraham kept the law, Paul demonstrates that God's way has always been the way of promise and faith.

3. Atonement. Christ came at the appointed time to redeem enslaved sinners (4:4–5) "by becoming a curse for us" (3:13).

4. Freedom. "It is for freedom that Christ has set us free" (5:1). Even those who are justified by faith in Christ sometimes find it easy to subject themselves to the slavery of a system.

5. Cross-centered life. No letter makes clearer than this one the importance of living out the implications of salvation through the cross.

G. Questions for Review and Discussion

1. Why did Paul write Galatians? How might you be prone to the two major errors that Paul refutes?

2. What contributions of Galatians do you find most applicable to your situation right now? Explain.

H. Recommended Resources

Introductory

Mahaney, C. J. *Living the Cross-Centered Life: Keeping the Gospel the Main Thing.* Sisters, OR: Multnomah, 2006.

Intermediate

Hansen, G. Walter. *Galatians.* IVPNTC. Downers Grove: InterVarsity Press, 1994.

Advanced

Carson, D. A. *The Letter to the Galatians.* PNTC. Grand Rapids: Eerdmans, forthcoming.

chapter thirteen

EPHESIANS

A. What Is Ephesians About?

1. After the opening greeting (1:1–2), Paul praises God for his predestining and redeeming activity in Christ—all to the praise of God's glorious grace (1:3–14). Fittingly, he then turns to thanksgiving and prayer for the letter's recipients (1:15–23).

2. Paul reminds the Ephesians of their sinfulness and of their salvation by grace through faith to do good works (2:1–10). Consequently, Christ brings peace and unity between Jews and Gentiles (2:11–22), a new oneness that Paul calls "the mystery of Christ" (3:1–6), which includes the way God's eternal purpose was worked out in Christ (3:7–13). This leads into a prayer for the readers (3:14–21).

3. Christians must keep "the unity of the Spirit" (4:1–6), appreciating the gifts of God to the church that enable growth in love (4:7–16). Exhortations to live as children of light include the highest theological incentives (4:17–5:21). The household code directs wives and husbands, children and parents, slaves and masters (5:22–6:9). Christians must put on the armor God provides (6:10–18), and Paul requests that they use the weapon of prayer on his behalf (6:19–20).

4. Paul closes with final greetings (6:21–24).

B. Who Wrote Ephesians?

The traditional view is that Ephesians is a genuine Pauline letter, but many modern scholars have denied this. Arguments such as the following support that Paul is the author:

1. It claims to have been written by Paul, not only in its opening (1:1) but also in the body of the letter (3:1). There are also many personal notes (1:15–16; 3:1; 4:1; 6:19–21).
2. It was widely circulated from early days, and its authenticity does not seem to have been doubted until recently.
3. Its structure, language, and themes parallel Paul's other letters.
4. It develops Colossians, which Paul wrote first. Paul may have written Colossians with a specific situation in mind and then written Ephesians with broader purposes.

C. Where Was Ephesians Written?

This letter seems to have been written from the same place as Colossians. (See further discussion in chapter 15.)

D. When Was Ephesians Written?

The letter speaks of Paul as in prison (3:1; 4:1). This is usually taken to refer to his first imprisonment in Rome toward the end of his life, which would mean a date in the early 60s.

E. To Whom Was Ephesians Written?

Although we might assume that this book was simply written to the church in Ephesus, there are two caveats we must consider:

1. The phrase "in Ephesus" is absent from 1:1 in some of the best manuscripts. (On the other hand, the phrase is included in nearly all manuscripts and by all the ancient versions; even the manuscripts that lack the phrase have "To the Ephesians" in the title.)
2. The calm and impersonal tone of the letter does not seem to befit Paul's relationship with the church at Ephesus. Paul had evangelized the Ephesians, spent a long time with them (Acts 19:8, 10; 20:31), and considered them his dear friends (Acts 20:17–38). Yet parts of this letter seem to indicate that the writer may not have personally interacted with the readers (e.g., 1:15; 3:2; 4:21).

These factors suggest another option for Ephesians: that Paul intended it to be a circular letter — that is, a letter intended to circulate among a general audience.

We do not, therefore, know with certainty that the letter was originally intended only for the church at Ephesus. The evidence of the great majority of the manuscripts and the improbabilities of other theories may compel us to take that view. If, on the other hand, we place great significance on the absence of Paul's characteristic warmth and of references to concrete situations, we are more likely to think of Ephesians as some form of a circular letter.

F. Why Was Ephesians Written?

Most of Paul's letters were written for a specific purpose on a specific occasion, but the occasion for Ephesians is unknown. Unlike Colossians, there is no specific false teaching against which Ephesians is aimed. Apparently, Paul thought his readers needed to be exhorted to pursue unity and a distinctively Christian ethic.

G. What Does Ephesians Contribute to Our Understanding of the Faith?

1. God's sovereignty in salvation. God chose believers before the creation of the world. They did not earn their salvation; God planned it in accordance with his pleasure and supreme will (1:3–11).
2. Christ's saving work. Blessings in Christ include sonship, redemption, and sealing with the Holy Spirit (1:5, 7, 13). He reconciles the universe (1:10) and Jews and Gentiles in the church (2:11–22; 3:10).
3. Christian growth in knowledge. What we could never work out for ourselves God has now made known. This is conveyed by the rich allusions to "mystery" (1:9; 3:3–11; 5:32; 6:19) and the concept of enlightenment (1:18; 4:18; 5:8–10, 17).
4. Love. The word *agape* ("love") occurs more often in Ephesians than in any other NT book except 1 Corinthians and 1 John. (See especially 3:17–19.)
5. Church. As the body and temple of Christ, the church occupies an important place in God's master plan (2:20–22). It is characterized by unity in diversity (2:11–3:6; 4:3–6, 11–13).
6. Transformed lives (4:1–6:18). Christians "must no longer live as the Gentiles do" (4:17). The contrast is like darkness and light (5:8). This has vital entailments for wives and husbands, children and parents, slaves and masters (5:22–6:9). Gospel-centered living by wearing God's armor is the only hope for Christians in the struggle against "spiritual forces of evil" (6:10–18).

H. Questions for Review and Discussion

1. What does Paul praise God for in 1:3–11?
2. John Newton, the former slave trader who wrote the hymn "Amazing Grace," reminisced at the end of his life, "My memory is nearly gone, but I remember two things: that I am a great sinner, and that Christ is a great Saviour" (see Josiah Bull, *The Life of John Newton* [1868; reprint, Edinburgh: Banner of Truth Trust, 2007]). What is the relationship between those "two things" (cf. 2:1–10)?
3. What implications does Paul's teaching on the church's unity have for you in your church situation?
4. Chapters 4–6 are filled with commands to Christians regarding how to live. What are some specific ways in which such a lifestyle is countercultural to your environment?

I. Recommended Resources

Intermediate

Liefeld, Walter L. *Ephesians.* IVPNTC. Downers Grove: InterVarsity Press, 1997.

Advanced

Hoehner, Harold W. *Ephesians: An Exegetical Commentary.* Grand Rapids: Baker, 2002.

O'Brien, Peter T. *The Letter to the Ephesians.* PNTC. Grand Rapids: Eerdmans, 1999.

chapter fourteen

PHILIPPIANS

A. What Is Philippians About?

1. After the customary opening greetings (1:1–2), Paul thanks God for the Philippians and prays for them (1:3–11). He notes that his imprisonment has advanced the gospel (1:12–18) and that he looks forward to being set free in response to their prayers (1:19–26).

2. Christians are called to suffer for Jesus (1:27–30) and must imitate the humility of Jesus, whom God exalted (2:1–11). They must "work out" their salvation (2:12–18).

3. Paul hopes to send Timothy to them soon and to come himself as well (2:19–24), and he updates them on Epaphroditus' health (2:25–30). He warns against people who were evidently advocating circumcision; he himself has had every reason for confidence in his life as a Jew, but knowing Christ is far more important (3:1–11). He is still pressing on toward the goal, and he invites the Philippians, as they anticipate Jesus' return, to join with him and not follow the "enemies of the cross of Christ" (3:12–4:1).

4. Paul pleads with two quarreling women to reconcile (4:2–3) and exhorts the Philippians to rejoice in the Lord, pray without anxiety and with the assurance that God's peace will guard them, and practice Christian virtues wholeheartedly (4:4–9). He thanks them for sending him gifts in his troubles (4:10–20).

5. He closes with greetings and a benediction (4:21–23).

B. Who Wrote Philippians?

The letter claims to have been written by Paul, and no serious doubt is raised against this claim. There are, however, a couple of related debates:

1. Some have recently suggested that Philippians is a composite of two or three of Paul's letters. More likely, however, it is simply one letter with abrupt changes of subject (e.g., 3:1 and 4:9).

2. Some contest the origin of the "hymn" in 2:5–11, which contains words and a rhythmic style that differ from Paul's other letters. The arguments are fairly evenly balanced as to whether Paul wrote the passage himself or borrowed it from something well-known in certain early churches. If Paul did not write the passage, there is no way of knowing who did. Moreover, if we assume that Paul quoted it, we must also assume that he did so because it says what *he* wanted to say — which means we still must interpret it within Paul's framework.

C. Where Was Philippians Written?

We know that Paul wrote this letter as a prisoner (1:7, 13, 17) with the possibility of imminent death (1:20; 2:17). He nonetheless anticipates a speedy release and looks forward to rejoining his Philippian friends (1:25–26; 2:23–24). What we do not know is the location of the prison. Paul was imprisoned on many occasions (2 Cor. 11:23), and he likely wrote Philippians from one of three places:

1. Rome: This is the traditional view, based partly on references to what is understood to be Paul's house arrest under the praetorian guard in Rome (1:13–14; 2:19, 25; 4:22; cf. Acts 28:16, 30–31). One problem is that the letter implies at least seven journeys by various people back and forth from Philippi, all within a relatively short timeframe. Since Philippi is about 1,200 miles from Rome, such journeys would take months; therefore it is more likely that Paul was imprisoned somewhere much closer to Philippi.

2. Caesarea: Paul was imprisoned here for two years (Acts 24:27) under Herod's praetorium (Acts 23:35). Caesarea, however, is about 1,000 miles from Philippi. Moreover, there is no evidence that a strong church (such as is depicted in Philippians) existed in Caesarea. There seems to be no convincing reason for holding this view.

3. Ephesus: There is no explicit statement that Paul was ever imprisoned in Ephesus, but Paul once had serious trouble there (1 Cor. 15:32; cf. 2 Cor. 1:8–11) that may have involved prison time. Philippi was only about 100 miles from Ephesus, where a unit of the praetorian guard was stationed.

The evidence suggests a strong but inconclusive case for Ephesus rather than Rome as the place of Paul's imprisonment.

D. When Was Philippians Written?

To date the letter, we must identify the imprisonment during which Paul wrote it. If he wrote it while imprisoned in Rome, we must date it about 61–62; if Caesarea, then perhaps 59–60; if Ephesus, then within the mid-50s to early 60s.

E. Why Was Philippians Written?

There does not seem to be one driving theme that we could identify as the purpose of this letter. Rather, Paul seems to have been prompted by a number of concerns, both personal and pastoral. Personal reasons for the letter include:

1. Updating the Philippians on how his situation is advancing the gospel (1:12–26)
2. Commending Timothy, possibly to prepare the way for his visit to Philippi (2:19–24)
3. Commending Epaphroditus for risking his life to take care of Paul's needs (2:25–30)
4. Thanking the Philippians for their gift (4:14–18)

   Some of Paul's broader pastoral concerns include:

1. Confronting two types of opponents: outsiders (1:28–30) and false teachers within the church (3:2–4, 18–19)
2. Calling attention to a need for unity (2:1–4; 4:2)
3. Emphasizing a need for wholehearted service (1:27–2:18)

These concerns, taken as a whole, may be considered the objective of this letter.

F. What Does Philippians Contribute to Our Understanding of the Faith?

1. Commendation. Many of Paul's other letters are consumed with correcting church problems, such as opposing false teaching and correcting lax practice. While Philippians has some gentle correction, its main thrust is commendation. Paul, on the whole, is delighted with their progress in the faith.
2. Jesus' humility and exaltation. The outstanding "hymn" in 2:6–11 highlights that Jesus, "in very nature God," condescended by taking the lowest place and dying on the cross to secure salvation. Now the Father has exalted him to the highest possible

place. As Jesus was vindicated, so also shall his people be, and that constitutes powerful incentive to press on (2:12–13). Moreover, this hymn—which may have been written even earlier than Philippians—constitutes powerful evidence for the confession of a high view of Christ at a very early date in the church's life.

3. Joy. A joyful note is sounded throughout this letter (the noun "joy" occurs five times and the verb "rejoice" nine times), emphasizing that Christians are a rejoicing people.

4. Gospel preaching. Paul encourages Christians who find others preaching the gospel with less than pure motives. What matters, he says, is that the gospel is preached (1:12–18).

5. Gospel partnership. The harmony between Paul and the Philippians illustrates working together for the sake of the gospel (1:5). Paul lovingly shepherds them, and they respond with maturity and affection.

6. Gospel suffering. Paul stresses the place of the cross and the resurrection in Christian salvation. Christian suffering is viewed as God's gift to advance the gospel (1:14–18, 29–30; 2:16–17). The important thing is serving Christ.

G. Questions for Review and Discussion

1. Why did Paul write Philippians?
2. For what specific actions and qualities does Paul commend the Philippians? What effect might this have had on the Philippians?
3. How are the contributions of Philippians connected with the gospel?

H. Recommended Resources

Introductory

Carson, D. A. *Basics for Believers: An Exposition of Philippians.* Grand Rapids: Baker, 1996.

Thielman, Frank. *Philippians.* NIVAC. Grand Rapids: Zondervan, 1995.

Advanced

Fee, Gordon D. *Paul's Letter to the Philippians.* NICNT. Grand Rapids: Eerdmans, 1995.

Hansen, G. Walter. *The Letter to the Philippians.* PNTC. Grand Rapids: Eerdmans, 2009.

chapter fifteen

COLOSSIANS

A. What Is Colossians About?

1. The opening greeting (1:1–2) is followed by thanksgiving and prayer for the Colossians (1:3–14).
2. Christ is supremely great (1:15–20). Paul relates Christ's reconciling work (1:21–23) to his own sufferings as he serves Christ (1:24–2:5), and he exhorts his readers to live in Christ and not be taken captive by "hollow and deceptive philosophy" (2:6–8). In light of Christ's greatness (2:9–15), they should not submit to people's ideas about food laws and religious festivals (2:16–23).
3. The way Christians live should evidence that they have been "raised with Christ" (3:1–17). This extends to the household code for wives and husbands, children and parents, slaves and masters (3:18–4:1). Christians should pray and be wise in their behavior toward outsiders (4:2–6).
4. Tychicus and Onesimus will bring the Colossians news of Paul, whose companions greet the Colossians (4:7–15). Archippus must exchange this letter with one to the Laodiceans so that each church may read both letters (4:16–17). The letter closes with a short form of Paul's usual ending (4:18).

B. Who Wrote Colossians?

The letter claims to have been written by Paul (1:1, 23; 4:18). Many scholars have recently argued that the author is instead a follower of Paul, and they dispute the letter's claim on three main grounds:

1. Its language and style are allegedly unlike Paul's. However, the minimal differences in vocabulary may be accounted for at least in part by the use of words needed to oppose a new heresy, and style differences could be attributed to the use of poetic forms.

2. Its theology is purportedly unlike Paul's. But this could be said of Paul's other letters as well. The absence of certain concepts and the presence of new ones (e.g., 1:16–20; 2:9–10, 12–13, 19; 3:1) can be attributed to a difference in audience and situation; they are not significant grounds for objection.
3. Its similarity to Ephesians elicits the argument that one person would never produce two letters so alike; rather, one author must have imitated the other. But it is quite reasonable to assume that Paul wrote both letters and simply repeated some of the same thoughts on two occasions for different audiences.

The objections to Paul's authorship of Colossians do not seem compelling, and his authorship is further supported by Colossians' links with Philemon.

C. Where Was Colossians Written?

Paul wrote this letter from prison (4:3, 10, 18), possibly from Ephesus, Caesarea, or Rome. The evidence favors Rome.

Ephesians, Colossians, and Philemon were probably written at the same time and from the same place, but Philippians (also written from prison) may have been written at a different time and place because it seems to have been written on a different occasion.

D. When Was Colossians Written?

If Paul wrote this letter from Rome, a date in the early A.D. 60s is likely, with 61 the most likely. If Paul wrote from a city other than Rome, a date in the late 50s is possible.

E. Why Was Colossians Written?

Paul writes Colossians primarily to refute the errors of some false teachers who had come to Colossae. The precise nature of the false teaching is not clear (as is common when we have none of the teaching itself, but only what is written to refute it). It appears to be a blend of Greek and Jewish teachings that minimized Christ (1:15–19; 2:9–10) and promoted asceticism (2:23), circumcision (2:11; 3:11), and observation of the Sabbath (2:16). Such a mixture of different religions was a feature of the ancient world, and it attracted new and imperfectly instructed Christians. Paul did not want the young church at Colossae to be harmed by these teachings.

F. What Does Colossians Contribute to Our Understanding of the Faith?

1. Christ's supremacy and atonement. According to the false teachers, elemental spirits were a barrier between God and his people, and only asceticism permitted access to God. But Christ is preeminent in everything, and he made peace by his work on the cross (1:15–20). Christ is uniquely excellent because of his saving cross-work (1:22, 27; 2:3, 9–10, 13–14, 20; 3:1, 11–12, 17).
2. Overcoming supernatural forces. The supreme Christ disarms all supernatural forces opposed to God's purpose (2:15). This is relevant today with rising occultism in the West.
3. Church unity. All believers form one church (3:11). Paul, who had never met the Colossians (2:1), exemplifies the love and tender concern that members of Christ's body should have for each other even when separated geographically.
4. Church diversity. Differences distinguish believers, so Paul gives specific directions to wives and husbands, children and parents, slaves and masters (3:18–4:1). All are servants of Christ, but that does not eliminate relationships in society.
5. Christ's headship. In every generation Christians are tempted to go along with the "hollow and deceptive philosophy" (2:8) of the times. Distracting religious practices undermine what is fundamental and generate a false humility and spirituality (2:16–23). Nothing can make up for losing connection with the head, Christ (1:15; 2:19).

G. Questions for Review and Discussion

1. What was the nature of the false teaching in Colossae, and how did Paul refute it?
2. What is the relationship between Christ's supremacy and atonement?
3. How does the connection that Christians have with Christ affect how they live now? (See especially 3:1–4:1.)

H. Recommended Resources

Introductory

Garland, David E. *Colossians/Philemon*. NIVAC. Grand Rapids: Zondervan, 1998.

Storms, Sam. *The Hope of Glory: 100 Daily Meditations on Colossians.* Wheaton: Crossway, 2008.

Intermediate

Wright, N. T. *Colossians and Philemon.* TNTC. Grand Rapids: Eerdmans, 1986.

Advanced

Moo, Douglas J. *The Letters to the Colossians and to Philemon.* PNTC. Grand Rapids: Eerdmans, 2008.

Thompson, Marrianne Meye. *Colossians and Philemon.* THNTC. Grand Rapids: Eerdmans, 2005.

chapter sixteen

1 AND 2 THESSALONIANS

A. What Are 1 and 2 Thessalonians About?

1 Thessalonians

1. The letter begins with the typical greeting (1:1), which mentions Paul, Silas, and Timothy as the senders. Paul thanks God for the Thessalonians and their commitment to the gospel (1:2–10).

2. Paul focuses on his interactions with the Thessalonians (2:1–3:13). He rehearses the circumstances of his gospel ministry in Thessalonica (2:1–12) and thanks God that the church there received God's word even though it involved suffering (2:13–16). This same persecution forced Paul to cut short his visit and aroused his fears that their courage might not endure this adversity (2:17–3:5), but Timothy has arrived to report that all is well (3:6–13).

3. Paul exhorts the Thessalonians (4:1–5:11). He reminds them of three ways they must "live in order to please God": avoid sexual immorality, love each other, and work hard with their own hands (4:1–12). Regarding those among them who have died, he encourages them with the advantages that the dead in Christ will have when the Lord returns (4:13–18). He exhorts them to lead exemplary lives in light of the coming day of the Lord (5:1–11).

4. The letter closes with final brief exhortations, a prayer-wish, a request for prayer, greetings, and a benediction (5:12–28).

2 Thessalonians

1. Paul again includes Silas and Timothy in the salutation (1:1–2), followed by thanksgiving and prayer to encourage the persecuted Thessalonians (1:3–12).

2. The persecution likely led the Thessalonians into erroneous ideas about the presence of the day of the Lord, which Paul corrects (2:1–12). He exhorts them to stand firm in their faith and prays that God would encourage them (2:13–17). He requests prayer for himself, Silas, and Timothy, that the Lord's word would spread rapidly through them and that God would protect them (3:1–5). The Thessalonians' erroneous belief about the presence of the day of the Lord probably worsened the problem of idleness, against which Paul again warns them (3:6–15; cf. 1 Thess. 4:11–12).

3. The letter ends with a brief prayer-wish, an authentication in Paul's own hand, and a benediction (3:16–18).

B. Who Wrote 1 and 2 Thessalonians?

This question involves three separate but related matters:

1. Co-authorship: Both letters name Paul, Silas, and Timothy as the authors, yet they are traditionally ascribed to Paul alone. Although the first-person plural (we, us) occurs in both letters, the first-person singular (I, me) does as well. Perhaps a mediating solution is the best: Silas and Timothy were closely associated with the letters, but Paul is the *primary* author; it is his voice that we hear.

2. Interruption of thought in 1 Thessalonians: Some argue that someone other than Paul inserted 2:13–16 into the letter, but these verses are present in every surviving manuscript and make good sense in their context.

3. Authorship of 2 Thessalonians: Paul attests his personal involvement at the end of this letter (3:17), and no responsible early church authority ever questioned Paul's authorship. But many modern scholars deny that Paul wrote the letter, advancing two major arguments:

   a. It is too *similar* to 1 Thessalonians; no author would duplicate material from one letter in another written so soon after and to the same audience. But these similarities are overdrawn.

b. It is too *different* from 1 Thessalonians in its word choices, formal tone, and teaching on the end times; the first letter emphasizes that Christ's return is imminent, and the second warns that certain "signs" will precede Christ's return. But the different pastoral situations explain this difference in focus. Certainly Paul could have held both views at the same time.

Since the reasons for rejecting Paul's authorship are not compelling and the evidence for pseudonymous letters is meager at best (see 2 Thess. 3:17 and ch. 8), 2 Thessalonians should be accepted as a genuine letter by Paul.

C. Where and When Were 1 and 2 Thessalonians Written?

Paul visited Thessalonica, a bustling commercial city in Macedonia of around 100,000 people, on his so-called second missionary journey, probably in A.D. 48 or 49 (Acts 17:1–9). Paul's short visit (Luke is vague about its length) caused such a disturbance in the city that he and Silas had to be sent away. Paul likely wrote 1 Thessalonians about four to six months later, in 50, while serving in Corinth; the occasion was Timothy's return from Thessalonica with good news about the church there (3:6). Paul likely wrote 2 Thessalonians very shortly after, either in late 50 or early 51.

Some suggest that Paul wrote 2 Thessalonians before 1 Thessalonians; however, their arguments are inconclusive. It can be inferred from 2 Thessalonians 2:15 that Paul had already written a letter to the Thessalonians, and the familial tone of 1 Thessalonians suggests an initial letter to a group of very recent converts.

D. Why Were 1 and 2 Thessalonians Written?

1 Thessalonians

First Thessalonians strengthens the faith of new converts:

1. Paul reminds the Thessalonians that they have been transformed by a powerful and reliable word from God (1:2–10).
2. Paul clears up any misconceptions about his own motives in light of his hasty departure from Thessalonica (chs. 2–3). He distances himself from immoral wandering teachers with impure motives, especially with regard to taking money.

3. Paul encourages them to hold fast to ethical implications of their new faith (4:1–12).
4. Paul comforts them over the death of some of their fellow Christians (4:13–5:11). They probably knew about both the resurrection of dead Christians and the rapture of living ones but did not know how to relate these to each other. They were distressed over the prospect that dead believers, although eventually raised, might miss out on the joyful reunion with the Lord at the time of his return.

2 Thessalonians

In 2 Thessalonians, Paul pursues the same basic purpose, focusing especially on the problems occasioned by a fresh outbreak of persecution. He puts this persecution into perspective with the end times (1:3–12) and deals with two issues that probably arose because of their suffering: their erroneous notion that the day of the Lord had arrived (2:1–12) and their tendency to idleness (3:6–15).

E. What Do 1 and 2 Thessalonians Contribute to Our Understanding of the Faith?

1. End times. When one thinks of the distinctive contribution of the Thessalonian letters, one thinks immediately of the branch of theology that deals with the "last things" or the end times ("eschatology"). This teaching is concentrated in 1 Thessalonians 4:13–5:11 and 2 Thessalonians 2:1–12.
   a. Deliverance. Jesus "rescues us from the coming wrath" (1 Thess. 1:10).
   b. Comfort. As a way of comforting the Thessalonians in light of their misunderstanding of the relationship between dead and living believers at the time of Christ's return, Paul goes into more detail than anywhere else on the precise sequence of events (4:13–18). When Jesus returns, God will regather all the saints with Jesus in a particular order: "the dead in Christ will rise first," and only then will those believers who are still alive be "caught up together with them in the clouds to meet the Lord in the air" (4:16-17).
   c. Timing of the resurrection. The resurrection of dead Christians will occur at Jesus' coming (4:13–16).

    d. Rapture. Living Christians will be snatched up to meet Christ when he returns (4:17).

    e. Imminency. Paul has the keen expectation that Christ's coming could occur within a very short period of time. The next paragraph (5:1–11) compares Christ's coming to the coming of a thief in the night (5:2). The unbeliever will be caught by surprise, so believers, knowing that the day of Christ's return is coming, will prepare themselves for it by living appropriately for the day that has already dawned (5:7–8).

    f. Already/not yet. The combination of the presence of the "Day" with its future coming reflects and contributes to the characteristic NT teaching that the kingdom of God is already inaugurated but not yet consummated. (This is known as "already/not yet" or "inaugurated eschatology.")

    g Judgment. God will judge those who are now tormenting the Thessalonians (2 Thess. 1:6–10).

    h. Events preceding Christ's coming. The day of the Lord, the time when God through Jesus intervenes to save his people and judge their enemies, will occur only after other preliminary events: the "rebellion" and the revelation of the man of lawlessness (2:3).

2. God's word. Paul refers to the word or message of the gospel in various ways nine times in 1 Thessalonians 1–2. The word is central (1:5–6, 8; 2:2, 4, 8–9, 13; cf. 2 Thess. 3:1), and faith is the natural and appropriate response. Paul emphasizes in these chapters that he did his best to get out of the way of the active, powerful word of God—to let it loose so that it would have its full impact.

3. God's family. The overall purpose of 1 Thessalonians is to strengthen the faith of new converts. Paul nurtures a young Christian community in the midst of a hostile and pluralistic environment—a situation not far off from that of the present-day church. He deals with many of the problems faced by new converts, such as alienation from family and friends and the cooling of one's initial spiritual ardor. The persecution that so had quickly arisen was an immediate and painful sign of the alienation that they were experiencing. Paul uses many familial images to remind them that their faith in Christ has introduced them into a new spiritual and eternal family. Paul himself has

acted as both mother and father to them (2:7, 11); Christians are "brothers and sisters" (2:1, 14, 17; 3:7; 4:1, 6, 10, 13; 5:1, 4, 12, 14, 25); and they need to exhibit toward each other the "brotherly love" that should typify family (4:9–10).

F. Questions for Review and Discussion

1. Why did Paul write 1 and 2 Thessalonians?
2. How is eschatology comforting?
3. How does eschatology provoke Christians to live now?

G. Recommended Resources

Introductory

Holmes, Michael W. *1 and 2 Thessalonians*. NIVAC. Grand Rapids: Zondervan, 1998.

Intermediate

Beale, G. K. *1–2 Thessalonians*. IVPNTC. Downers Grove: Inter-Varsity Press, 2003.

Advanced

Green, Gene L. *The Letters to the Thessalonians*. PNTC. Grand Rapids: Eerdmans, 2002.

Morris, Leon. *The First and Second Epistles to the Thessalonians*. Rev. ed. NICNT. Grand Rapids: Eerdmans, 1991.

chapter seventeen

1 AND 2 TIMOTHY AND TITUS

The letters to Timothy and Titus are usually grouped together as "the Pastoral Epistles," a title apparently given to them in the early 1700s. The title is appropriate because they are the only NT letters addressed to individuals responsible for pastoring and appointing pastors.

A. What Are the Pastoral Epistles About?

1 Timothy

1. The short greeting mentions "God our Savior" (1:1–2).
2. Paul warns against false teachers of the law who promote controversies rather than advance God's work (1:3–11). He thanks Christ for the grace and mercy at work in him (1:12–17) and purposes to help Timothy fight the battle well (1:18–20).
3. Paul urges prayer for all, especially those in authority so that they may promote conditions conducive for Christian growth and evangelism (2:1–7). He moves from prayer in the right spirit (2:8) to the way women should dress and live (2:9–15) to qualifications for overseers (3:1–7), deacons (3:8–10, 12–13), and either deacons' wives or female deacons (3:11). He explains his concern for God's household (3:14–16).
4. Paul further warns against false teachers (4:1–5) and exhorts Timothy to persevere as a good servant of Christ (4:6–16). He explains how to treat older and younger men and women (5:1-2), widows (5:3-16), and elders (5:17–20), charging Timothy to avoid partiality (5:21). He adds some further pastoral advice (5:22–25) and an admonition that slaves should respect their masters (6:1–2).

5. Paul again warns against false teachers and the love of money (6:3–10). Timothy must flee from all such conduct and live above reproach (6:11–16). Rich people must lay up treasure that matters by doing good (6:17–19).

6. Paul ends with another exhortation to be firm in the faith and a grace wish (6:20–21).

2 Timothy

Paul wrote this while contemplating his own approaching death (4:6–8), so it has a special solemnity.

1. After a typical greeting (1:1–2), Paul thanks God for Timothy (1:3–5).

2. Paul encourages Timothy (1:6–7) and exhorts him not to be ashamed of Paul, because Paul is not ashamed of the gospel (1:8–14). He shares some bad and good examples of loyalty (1:15–18).

3. Paul urges Timothy to be strong in Christ's grace (2:1–7) and reminds him of the essentials of the gospel (2:8–13). Timothy must be a faithful, unashamed workman who opposes false teaching and lives uprightly (2:14–26).

4. Paul prophesies of troubles "in the last days," when all sorts of evil flourishes (3:1–9). The Lord has protected Paul in his troubles (3:10–13), and Paul exhorts Timothy to continue in the teaching he has had from infancy—specifically the teaching from the Scriptures, which are God-breathed and valuable (3:14–17). Timothy must preach the word steadfastly (4:1–5).

5. Paul is prepared for his impending death (4:6–8). He makes some personal remarks (4:9–18) and closes with greetings and a benediction (4:19–22).

Titus

1. The lengthy opening greeting reminds Titus that God has promised eternal life and brought it to pass in due course (1:1–4).

2. Paul has left Titus in Crete to set things in order in the church, and he now urges him to appoint qualified elders in every town (1:5–9). Paul warns Titus against the "many rebellious people" in Crete (1:10–16).

3. Titus must teach those in his church how to live. Paul details specific instructions for older men (2:2), older women, who will

in turn teach younger women (2:3–5), young men (2:6–8), and slaves (2:9–10). All believers must live uprightly, awaiting the glorious appearing "of our great God and Savior, Jesus Christ" (2:11–15).

4. Christians must obey authorities (3:1–2). Paul contrasts the way believers lived before salvation with the way they should live as Christians (3:3–8). He exhorts them to avoid foolish divisions (3:9–11).

5. Paul closes with instructions about various individuals followed by greetings and a benediction (3:12–15).

B. Who Wrote 1 and 2 Timothy and Titus?

The Pastoral Epistles share similarities, but nothing conclusively demonstrates that they were written at the same time or from the same place. Most modern critical scholars hold that the Pastoral Epistles are pseudonymous, that is, the author is not Paul but someone addressing the people of his own day with what he thought Paul would have said to them. (On pseudonymous letters, see chapter 8.) Their arguments denying Paul's authorship include the following:

1. Vocabulary and syntax: It can be argued that the Pastoral Epistles' words and arrangement of words ("syntax") are too different from Paul's other letters. These epistles do, in fact, contain 306 words not found elsewhere in Paul's writings; however, this is not in itself a reason to doubt his authorship. Since most of those words are known to have been current in his day, it is reasonable to suppose that Paul would have used them. The distinct vocabulary and syntax of these three books could be explained by a variety of factors, including different scribes, different topics, and different audiences (pastors rather than churches) with specific challenges.

2. Rhetorical style: Some contend that the style of argument and the composition of the Pastoral Epistles are too different from Paul's other letters. However, it is reasonable to expect a range of expression from one author writing across a span of nearly a quarter of a century, especially when that author is writing to individuals and groups as diverse as those represented by Paul's letters.

3. Historical problems: It is difficult to harmonize the Pastoral Epistles' historical situation with Paul's life as recorded in Acts and Paul's other letters. On the other hand, all the historical references in these letters are accurate and consistent with Paul's lifetime.

      a. These events likely occurred after Paul's first imprisonment in Rome (Acts 28) and before he was martyred in Rome.

      b. The historical data in the Pastorals *could* fit within the confines of Paul's known ministry up to his first Roman imprisonment, since there are huge gaps when other events could be squeezed in.

      c. Denying Paul's authorship does not adequately account for all the personal reminiscences reflecting real history (e.g., 1 Tim. 1:3; 3:14–15; 2 Tim. 1:16–17; 4:13; Titus 3:13).

4. Additional historical conflicts: The Pastoral Epistles seem to refute a false teaching (Gnosticism) that was an issue only after Paul died. Moreover, they are seen by some as presupposing a strongly organized church structure (e.g., an ordained ministry) that did not exist during the time of his ministry. Neither of these points, however, presents a strong case against Paul's authorship. All the false teaching described in these letters fits into what is known during the time of Paul's ministry (cf. Colossians). Regarding church organization, it can be argued that these letters call for no more organization than the "overseers and deacons" of Philippians 1:1.

5. Theology: The Pastoral Epistles contain Greek terms for salvation that some scholars doubt Paul would have used. But a closer look reveals that these expressions often incorporate words and phrases that Paul uses elsewhere; additionally, many other terms in these letters are consistent with Paul's other writings.

C. Where and When Were the Pastoral Epistles Written?

1 Timothy and Titus

Paul likely wrote these letters around the same period, after being released from his first imprisonment in Rome. This would date them in the early to middle A.D. 60s.

Not enough is known to identify the places of origin with certainty, as Paul was engaged in missionary activity during this time. The best suggestion is that 1 Timothy was written from Macedonia (1:3). Titus was probably written while he was in or en route to Nicopolis, where he planned to spend the winter (3:12).

2 Timothy

Paul probably wrote this letter during his second imprisonment in Rome while facing the prospect of imminent execution (1:16–17;

4:6). This would put the date of writing in the A.D. 60s, probably about 64 or 65.

D. To Whom and Why Were the Pastoral Epistles Written?

Paul was Timothy's mentor. His first letter gives Timothy the guidance he needs for his work as a superintendent of churches. The second is so personal that it is probably the hardest of the three Pastorals to claim as pseudonymous (cf. 1:4–6, 15–18; 2:1–2, 22–26; 3:14-15; 4:2, 5, 9–22).

Titus was written to a trusted helper whom Paul expects to act responsibly (1:4; 3:12–15).

E. What Do These Epistles Contribute to Our Understanding of the Faith?

1 Timothy

1. Mentoring. Paul mentored Timothy and grew very fond of him (cf. 1 Cor. 4:17; Phil. 2:20; 1 Thess. 3:2). Paul compares Timothy to a son (Phil. 2:22; 1 Tim. 1:2; cf. 1 Thess. 3:2) and links him with his own ministry in the opening greetings of six letters (2 Cor.; Phil.; Col.; 1–2 Thess.; Phlm.). Christians are joined in the Lord's service, and there is significant help they can and should give to one another.

2. Church leadership. Those in the ministry must be above reproach (3:2-13); they must carefully avoid the snare of focusing on church activities rather than character. "Overseer" (3:1–7) appears to be an alternative title for "elder" (5:17–19; cf. Titus 1:5–7) or "pastor." Women, Paul insists, have a different role and must not teach or exercise authority over men (2:11-13). One qualification not required of deacons (3:8–12) is the ability to teach (cf. 3:2).

3. Christian living. All Christians must live uprightly (3:14–15), but there are different duties for those with different roles: women (2:9–15), older and younger people (5:1–2), widows (5:3–16), slaves (6:1–2), and the wealthy (6:17–19).

4. Needless controversy. Christians must avoid unnecessary controversies (1:4; 4:3, 7; 6:4–5).

5. Money. Paul's warnings against people who "think that godliness is a means to financial gain" (6:5) are particularly relevant in our money-driven culture. The modern-day church must be

careful to heed his admonition that the "love of money is a root of all kinds of evil" (6:10).

6. Gospel-centrality. Sound doctrine is grounded in the essentials of the gospel (1:10b-11; 2:5–7), and whatever the circumstances in which Timothy finds himself, he must proclaim the gospel, which is central to the life of the whole Christian church.

2 Timothy

1. Martyrdom. Paul was about to be executed for holding the Christian faith (4:6–8). He writes in the shadow of the scaffold, and his last communication to a trusted subordinate shows what he considers to be important. He shows us how a Christian martyr should face death. (This is highly relevant to our day, as there have been more Christian martyrs during the past 150 years than in the previous eighteen centuries combined.) Paul calmly contemplates what lay ahead, and quiet faith undergirds all he does. He displays no fanaticism, no grandstanding.

2. The non-negotiable gospel. The foundation of all Christian life is what God has already done, and Christians must live out the consequences of God's saving act. Believers are not merely given a list of instructions as to what constitutes the path of the service of God and then left to try to work it all out themselves. Paul's teaching must be passed on as long as this world lasts (2:2). The essence of the Christian faith is not open to negotiation. God has spoken, and we neglect what he has said to our peril (3:16–17).

3. Sacrificial service. The cost of discipleship may be great and often includes suffering (1:8, 12; 2:9, 12; 3:11–12). Christian service is comparable to that of a soldier, athlete, and hardworking farmer (2:3–6). While salvation is a free gift from God, it is also demanding. In living out its implications, the believer will inevitably experience difficulties and will find that the God who sent his Son to die on the cross is always served at a cost.

4. Opposition. Christians meet with opposition, sometimes from other professing Christians, and Paul warns against those who wander from the truth (2:14–18; 3:1–5; 4:3). Sound, solid teaching is vital (1:13; 2:19).

Titus

1. Gospel transformation. This letter brings out something of what we might call the civilizing function of Christianity. Titus was in

charge of appointing elders for a very young church in very bleak cultural surroundings (cf. 1:12). This indicates that the church is not intended to function only in cozy, respectable, middle-class environments; rather, the gospel is for even those who seem most unpromising. This is also seen in the instructions to converts (2:3–4, 10; 3:1–2), which indicate Paul's expectation that the Cretans develop the qualities of Christian character despite their dubious background.

2. Evangelism despite opposition. Christian teachers must press on with the gospel regardless of the strength and the nature of the opposition from rival teachers (1:10–16; 3:9–11).

3. God's grace. Paul takes no position of superiority; he owes everything to "the kindness and love of God our Savior" and specifically to what God has done in Christ (3:3–7). He puts the highest standard before the Cretans, for "the grace of God has appeared that offers salvation to all people" (2:11). The Christian approach urges people to rely not on themselves but rather on the grace of God, which "teaches" them how to live (2:12).

4. Christ's coming. Paul waits for the culmination of what God has done in Christ: "the blessed hope—the appearing of the glory of our great God and Savior, Jesus Christ" (2:13).

F. Questions for Review and Discussion

1. What are some themes common to all three letters?
2. How does Paul's situation in 2 Timothy differ from the other two letters?
3. Why are these letters particularly helpful for church leaders?

G. Recommended Resources

Intermediate

Köstenberger, Andreas J. "The Pastoral Epistles." Pages 487–625 in *Ephesians–Philemon*. Rev. ed. EBC 12. Grand Rapids: Zondervan, 2006.

Towner, Philip H. *1–2 Timothy and Titus*. IVPNTC. Downers Grove: InterVarsity Press, 1994.

Advanced

Towner, Philip H. *The Letters to Timothy and Titus*. NICNT. Grand Rapids: Eerdmans, 2006.

chapter eighteen

PHILEMON

A. What Is Philemon About?

1. Paul opens with a typical greeting and thanksgiving (vv. 1–7).
2. Paul delicately appeals to Philemon for "my son Onesimus," a slave whom Paul apparently evangelized and who may now live up to the meaning of his name: "useful" (vv. 8–11).
3. Paul wants Philemon, Onesimus's master, to be reconciled with Onesimus as a brother—no longer as a slave—and then allow Onesimus to return and join Paul in ministry (vv. 12–16).
4. Paul repeats his request that Philemon welcome Onesimus as a fellow believer and adds that he will repay Philemon for any losses incurred because of Onesimus (vv. 17–19). Paul implies that he was instrumental in Philemon's conversion.
5. Paul ends the body of the letter with a final appeal (v. 20; cf. v. 7).
6. Paul expresses confidence that Philemon will do even more than Paul asks, perhaps a hint that Philemon should grant Onesimus his freedom (vv. 20–21). He closes with his travel plans, greetings, and a benediction (vv. 22–25).

B. Who Wrote Philemon?

Contemporary scholars unanimously view Paul as the author.

C. Where and When Was Philemon Written?

Paul likely wrote Colossians and Philemon at the same place and time: probably Rome in the early 60s. Both letters include Timothy as the co-sender; depict Paul in prison; refer to Epaphras and Archippus; include Mark, Aristarchus, Demas, and Luke among Paul's companions; and refer to Onesimus. Since Onesimus was a resident of Colossae (Col. 4:9), we are safe in assuming that Philemon was also.

D. To Whom and Why Was Philemon Written?

Philemon is the shortest and most personal of all Paul's letters. More than just a personal note between two people (vv. 1–2), it falls somewhere between a simple private letter and a public letter intended for a broad audience.

Paul writes to Philemon—whom we know only as a "slave owner" in whose home the church meets (v. 2)—about a sensitive matter, and there are at least two viable views explaining why:

1. Onesimus was Philemon's runaway slave and was converted after encountering Paul, who was imprisoned in Rome. Paul, in conformity with Roman law, is sending Onesimus back to his master. Paul delicately writes Philemon to explain the situation, encouraging Philemon to accept Onesimus back as a brother and perhaps even set him free. This traditional explanation suffers from one key difficulty: How was it that Onesimus just happened to run into a man in prison who knew his own master? One possible answer is that Onesimus, having successfully fled as far as Rome, might have had second thoughts about his escape and sought out Paul for refuge and assistance.

2. Onesimus was not a runaway slave, but a slave who had poor standing with his master and sought Paul's help to mediate. It is unlikely, however, that Onesimus would have gone as far as Rome—if that is where Paul was—to find a mediator.

E. What Does Philemon Contribute to Our Understanding of the Faith?

1. Sacrificial love. The letter is a beautiful picture of the mutual love and respect that should characterize the body of Christ at work. Each of the three key characters must sacrifice his own interest for the interests of fellow believers (cf. Phil. 2:4):

    a. Onesimus must return to his master and resubmit to his authority (and possibly punishment).

    b. Paul, by refusing to exercise his apostolic authority, puts himself in the role of a Christian appealing to a fellow Christian.

      c. Philemon is encouraged to act out of Christian love, not because Paul demands it. Paul subtly pressures Philemon (partly because Onesimus is so dear to Paul) but still leaves Philemon's options open.

2. Slavery. The letter contributes to our understanding of the Christian approach to slavery. Paul does not attack the institution of slavery, either here or elsewhere in his letters — the NT writers simply do not deal with institutions in these ways. Paul is clear that Onesimus's conversion puts him into an entirely new relationship to his owner, and Paul is clearly saying that Philemon should at least treat Onesimus as a brother even though he is still Philemon's slave. But is he saying more than this? It is not certain, but it may well be that he is also hinting at the social implications of Onesimus's new spiritual status: Philemon should no longer consider Onesimus his slave since they are now brothers.

F. Questions for Review and Discussion

1. In your own words, explain what this letter is about.
2. Why do you think that this letter is in the Bible? What is its permanent value?

G. Recommended Resources

See the resources cited for Colossians.

chapter nineteen

HEBREWS

A. What Is Hebrews About?

The theme of Hebrews is that Jesus Christ is supreme. His unqualified supremacy tolerates no challenge, whether from angels or humans: his inaugurated covenant is superior to any that preceded it; his priesthood is better than Levi's; the sacrifice he has offered is superior to those offered under the Mosaic code; the OT's very purpose was to anticipate and point to him. Weaving exposition and exhortation throughout the letter, the author emphasizes Christ's supremacy as he warns readers not to turn back from the Christian faith (2:1–4; 3:7–4:11; 4:14–16; 5:11–6:12; 10:19–39; 12:1–13:17).

1. God's revelation by his Son, Jesus Christ, is superior and final (1:1–4). The Son is superior to angels (1:5–14). Warning: Do not drift away from this superior revelation, especially since God severely judged those who ignored the earlier, lesser revelation (2:1–4). Jesus has identified himself with mortal, fallen humans (not angels) as their "merciful and faithful high priest" (2:5–18).
2. Both Moses and Jesus faithfully served in God's household, but Jesus is "worthy of greater honor than Moses" (3:1–6). Warning: Do not fall away into unbelief and miss God's rest as many of Moses' generation did (3:7–4:11). Trying to escape the perceptive authority of this revelation is utter folly (4:12–13).
3. Jesus is the great high priest: he can empathize with our weaknesses (4:14–16), and he superlatively meets the qualifications that applied to the high priests of the old covenant (5:1–10). Warning: Do not fall away (5:11–6:20). Move beyond spiritual immaturity (5:11–6:3). Since apostates cannot be recovered (6:5–8), persevere in light of the certainty of God's promise (6:9–20).

4. The Melchizedekian priesthood is superior to the Levitical priesthood, and Jesus belongs to the former (7:1–28; cf. 5:6, 10; Gen. 14:18–20; Ps. 110). Unlike the sacrifices of the old covenant, which "made nothing perfect" (7:19), Jesus' sacrifice is permanently effective, "able to save completely those who come to God through him" (7:25). The high priest and tabernacle of the obsolete old covenant are but shadows of the new covenant's high priest: Jesus (8:1–13; cf. Jer. 31:31–34). Worship in the tabernacle (9:1–10) contrasts with the permanent effect of Christ's sacrifice (9:11–28). The old order was "only a shadow" of the new covenant's reality (10:1–10). Even the new high priest's enthronement attests the finality and permanent effectiveness of his sacrificial work (10:11–18).

5. Warning: Persevere! Turning aside is profoundly dangerous in light of the new covenant's exclusive sufficiency (10:19–39). Persevering faith is required and is modeled throughout Scripture (11:1–40). Look to Jesus, who "pioneered" our faith by opening up the way to God and "perfected" it by completing all that was necessary (12:1–3). Trials are discipline from God's loving hand (12:4–11). Those who fall away align themselves with Esau (12:12–17). The earthly Sinai of the old covenant contrasts with the heavenly Zion, to which Christians come — so persevere (12:18–29).

6. The concluding exhortations counter particular ways in which the readers might backslide (13:1–17). The author concludes with a request for prayer (13:18–19), his own prayer and doxology (13:20–21), some personal notes (13:22–23), and final greetings and a benediction (13:24–25).

B. Who Wrote Hebrews?

We do not know who wrote Hebrews. Paul has been suggested as the author, but this is highly unlikely. Vocabulary and stylistic differences abound, and although these cannot by themselves disprove Paul's authorship, they do make it a less plausible alternative. More significant is the absence of a self-identifying greeting at the beginning of the letter, as it was Paul's normal practice to include such a greeting. Above all, it is almost impossible to believe that Paul would identify himself as one of those who heard the gospel, not from the Lord, but from "those who heard him" (2:3; cf. Gal. 1:11–12). Today virtually no one defends Pauline authorship.

Other suggested authors include Barnabas, Apollos, Aquila and Priscilla, Silas, Timothy, Epaphras, the deacon Philip, Mary the mother of Jesus, Luke, and Clement of Rome. Rather than speculate, it is far better to admit that we simply do not know who wrote Hebrews. We do know that the author was well-versed in the Greek Old Testament, as evidenced by the fact that none of his numerous quotations depend on the Hebrew OT. He was likely a well-educated Greek Jew who had become a Christian, a second-generation believer (Heb. 2:3). His identity was almost certainly known to the first readers of Hebrews.

C. Where Was Hebrews Written?

We have even less evidence about where Hebrews was written. The only explicit clue is found in 13:24: "Those from Italy send you their greetings." The expression is unclear: it could indicate that the letter was written to or from Italy — or it could indicate neither. Any analysis of the book and its conceptual categories will probably reveal more about the work's intended readers than about its writing.

D. When Was Hebrews Written?

Although any date between about A.D. 60 and 100 is plausible, the preponderance of evidence favors a date before A.D. 70. This is supported by the fact that sacrifices in Jerusalem ceased after Rome destroyed the temple in 70. The author gives the impression that sacrifices were still occurring when he wrote this letter (e.g., 8:13; 10:1 – 3); if sacrifices had already ceased, the author's argument would have had to be cast in a different form.

E. To Whom and Why Was Hebrews Written?

Any assessment of the purpose of Hebrews is inextricably tied to one's understanding of the identity of the addressees. Because the author refers to experiences in the lives of his readers (e.g., 10:32 – 34), we can assume that he has a specific group in mind as he writes. Suggestions for this group's location include Alexandria, Antioch, Bithynia and Pontus, Caesarea, Colossae, Corinth, Cyprus, Ephesus, Jerusalem (or Palestine in general), Rome, and Samaria. While Rome may seem to be the most likely choice, any attempt to pinpoint the location is merely conjecture. Fortunately, few exegetical issues depend on determining the geographic location of the addressees.

All agree that the book is written for Christians who are urged to maintain their confession (e.g., 3:6, 14; 4:14; 10:23), but not all agree as to whether their ethnic background is Greek or Jewish. The author hints at why the readers might revert to some form of Judaism (e.g., 13:7–9, 13), but it is not so much the *reasons* that interest the author as the *outcome*: as they relativize Christ's sacrifice and priestly work, they effectively deny them — and in so doing come dangerously close to apostasy. The author writes this letter to prevent just such a calamity.

F. What Style of Literature Is Hebrews?

Hebrews is one of only two New Testament letters which begin without a greeting and without naming the writer and intended audience. (The other is 1 John.) Yet it concludes like a letter (13:20–25), and the author has specific readers in mind (cf. 5:12; 6:10; 10:32). It probably was originally a sermon or series of sermons turned into a letter.

The structure of the book continues to be the subject of much scholarly debate, but its message comes through with clarity.

G. What Does Hebrews Contribute to Our Understanding of the Faith?

1. Christ's person and work. Hebrews enriches our understanding of Jesus' priestly work, the finality of his sacrifice, the nature of his sonship, the importance of the incarnation, and his role as "pioneer" of our faith. Connected themes that are prominent in Hebrews include perfection (e.g., 7:11, 19, 28), Sabbath-rest (4:1-11), faith (ch. 11), and the new covenant (e.g., 8:6–13).

2. Model for interpretation. The author's extensive use of the OT enables us to explore how first-century Christians read the OT. Within Hebrews we find typology, prophecy, and the interplay between specific OT texts and the history of the Hebrew people. In this way, Hebrews provides many working elements for reading the Bible inductively, holistically, and historically, and for interpreting specific scriptures within the constraints of the history of salvation.

3. People of God. It sheds light on our understanding of how the people of God moved from Israel (under the old covenant) to the church (under the new covenant).

4. Perseverance. Hebrews exhorts Christians to persevere, giving a clear warning against apostasy and the comfort provided by religious externalism.

H. Questions for Review and Discussion

1. According to Hebrews, Jesus Christ is better than what? Why?
2. Professing Christians should beware of what?
3. What is new about the new covenant?

I. Recommended Resources

Introductory

Guthrie, George H. *Hebrews*. NIVAC. Grand Rapids: Zondervan, 1998.

Hagner, Donald A. *Encountering the Book of Hebrews: An Exposition*. Grand Rapids: Baker, 2002.

Intermediate

France, R. T. "Hebrews." Pages 17–195 in *Hebrews–Revelation*. Rev. ed. EBC 13. Grand Rapids: Zondervan, 2006.

Advanced

O'Brien, Peter T. *The Letter to the Hebrews*. PNTC. Grand Rapids: Eerdmans, 2010.

chapter twenty

JAMES

A. What Is James About?

1. The opening addresses "the twelve tribes scattered among the nations" (1:1).
2. Trials and maturity (1:2–18). Christians must find meaning and purpose in their suffering (1:2–4) and pray in faith for wisdom (1:5–8). A Christian worldview should be applied to poverty and wealth (1:9–11) and trials and temptation (1:12–15). God is the source of every good gift (1:16–18).
3. True Christianity is seen in its works (1:19–2:26). This section focuses on three related words:
   a. "Word [of God]" (especially 1:19–27). "Accept the word planted in you" (1:21) and truly receive God's word by *doing* it (1:22–27), such as avoiding loose speech and anger (1:19–20).
   b. "Law" (especially 2:1–13). Christians will fulfill the "royal law" and escape judgment by being impartial in their treatment of others.
   c. "Deeds" (especially 2:14–26). True faith is always marked by obedience, and only such faith evidenced in works will bring salvation.
4. Community dissensions (3:1–4:12). Beware the power and danger of the tongue (3:1–12). Dissensions result from the wrong kind of wisdom (3:13–18) and frustrated desires (4:1–3). Repent of compromised Christianity (4:4–10), and do not slander or judge one another (4:11–12).
5. Implications of a Christian worldview (4:13–5:11). Take God into account in all your plans (4:13–17). God will judge the wicked rich (5:1–6) and reward the righteous (5:7–11) when the Lord returns.
6. Concluding exhortations (5:12–20). Do not take oaths (5:12); pray, especially for physical healing (5:13–18); and look after one another's spiritual health (5:19–20).

B. Who Wrote James?

The letter claims to have been written by "James, a servant of God and of the Lord Jesus Christ" (1:1). An unknown James is possible, but the simplicity of the author's identification points to a well-known individual, likely one mentioned in the NT. Possible authors include the following:

1. James the son of Zebedee, brother of John, and one of the Twelve (e.g., Mark 1:19; 5:37; 9:2; 10:35; 14:33) was martyred in about 44 (Acts 12:2), probably too early to write this letter.
2. James the son of Alphaeus, also one of the Twelve (Mark 3:18, perhaps 15:40), is too obscure.
3. James the father of Judas (Luke 6:16; Acts 1:13) is even more obscure.
4. A pseudonymous author (an unknown early Christian writing in the name of James) is argued by some, but this faces serious objections regarding the acceptability of pseudonymous letters in the ancient world. (See ch. 8.)
5. It is widely accepted that the author is James the brother of Jesus ("the Lord's brother," Gal. 1:19), who played a leading role in the early Jerusalem church and is certainly the most prominent James in the NT (see Acts 12:17; 15:13; 21:18). This is the natural implication of the letter's own claims, it is corroborated by NT and early Christian evidence, and there are no decisive arguments against it.

C. Where and When Was James Written?

James probably wrote this letter from Jerusalem during his tenure as leader of the Christian church in Jerusalem. Some who identify the author as James the brother of Jesus date the letter shortly before his martyrdom in A.D. 62. One argument for this late date is that it would take some time for Paul's letters to become sufficiently well known before James could respond to their content, as he seems to be doing in 2:14–26. But this passage makes better sense as a response not to Paul's writings themselves but to an indirect, inaccurate form of Paul's teaching that uses justification by faith alone as an excuse for moral laxity. Thus it can be argued that James wrote his letter *before* hearing Paul or reading any of his letters—that is, while Paul's teaching on justification was beginning to have an impact on the church, yet before Paul could discuss it with James at the Jerusalem Council in 48 or 49 (Acts 15). This more likely scenario would place the letter around 46–48, a date that nicely fits the circumstances and emphases of the letter.

D. To Whom Was James Written?

As early as the fourth century, the seven letters that follow Hebrews in the NT were known as the Catholic (i.e., universal) Epistles because, unlike Paul's letters, they appeared to be addressed to the church in general rather than to a single congregation. But each of these letters was written, if not to a single congregation, at least to people in a specific geographical area.

While addressed generally to "the twelve tribes scattered among the nations" (1:1), James is probably intended for a limited number of Jewish Christians (cf. 1:25; 2:2, 8–13; perhaps Acts 11:19) to the north and east of Palestine. James sends consolation and exhortation to the dispersed covenant people of God. But the category of "catholic" or "general" letter still fits James in the sense that it lacks any reference to specific local issues or persons.

E. What Style of Literature Is James?

Although the letter has a typical introduction, it lacks a typical closing (e.g., travel plans, prayer requests, greetings). This suggests that James is a more formal letter, intended for communities in which James's scattered parishioners had settled. More specifically, the letter is likely a sermon or series of sermons.

1. Pastoral admonition pervades the letter. Commands occur with greater frequency in James than in any other NT book.
2. Its structure is loose, moving rapidly from topic to topic, often changing subjects after only a few verses.
3. It extensively and effectively uses metaphors and figures of speech (e.g., billowing sea, withered flower, brushfire).

F. What Does James Contribute to Our Understanding of the Faith?

1. Faith and works. James's primary contribution is his insistence that genuine Christian faith must become evident in works. He resolutely opposes the common tendency among Christians to be content with a half-hearted, compromising faith that seeks to have the best of both this world and the next. This is the sin of double-mindedness (1:8; 4:8), and James insists that Christians repent of it.
2. Justification and works. James's emphasis on the role of works in justification (2:14–26) creates potential conflict with Paul's

insistence that justification comes by faith alone (e.g., Rom. 3:28). We may harmonize James with Paul in at least two different ways:

a. James is using the verb "justify" in the sense of "vindicate before people" (e.g., Luke 7:29). Paul refers to the *declaration* of our righteousness, but James to the *demonstration* of our righteousness.

b. James is using the verb "justify" in the sense of "vindicate at the last judgment" (e.g., Matt. 12:37). Both Paul and James are referring to the sinner's righteousness before God, but Paul focuses on the initial reception of that status while James emphasizes the way that status is vindicated before God in the judgment. Justification is by faith "from first to last" (Rom. 1:17), but because true biblical faith is powerful and active (James 5:16), true believers will produce those works necessary for vindication on the last day.

While such theological harmonization is absolutely necessary, it should not lead us to ignore the important contribution made either by Paul or James. Paul and James are combating different opponents while fighting back-to-back. Paul combats the attempt to base salvation on human works (legalism), and James combats the attitude that dismisses works as unnecessary for Christians.

G. Questions for Review and Discussion

1. How is James different than a typical letter?
2. Summarize what James says about (1) trials and (2) speech.
3. How do you harmonize James 2:14–26 (justification by faith *and* works) with Paul's justification by faith alone?

H. Recommended Resources

Intermediate

Guthrie, George H. "James." Pages 197–273 in *Hebrews–Revelation*. Rev. ed. EBC 13. Grand Rapids: Zondervan, 2006.

Advanced

Bauckham, Richard. *James: Wisdom of Jesus, Disciple of Jesus the Sage*. London: Routledge, 1999.

Moo, Douglas J. *The Letter of James*. PNTC. Grand Rapids: Eerdmans, 2000.

chapter twenty-one

1 PETER

A. What Is 1 Peter About?

Unlike Paul, who often develops a theological point before applying it, Peter mixes doctrine and application. Nearly every paragraph
opens with a command, which is then grounded by theology brought
in along the way.

1. The opening calls Christians "God's elect" and refers to them as
   scattered exiles (1:1–2).
2. God's people have privileges and responsibilities (1:3–2). Their
   new birth provides for them a secure hope and inheritance —
   future salvation (1:3–9). The prophets predicted this salvation, and angels themselves long to understand it (1:10–12).
   Christians must exhibit a holy lifestyle rooted in their new
   birth and stimulated by God's act of redeeming them in Christ
   (1:13–2:3). The metaphor of Christ as "stone" reminds Christians of their new status: God's people, destined to declare his
   praises (2:4–10).
3. Christians must live like aliens and strangers in the world
   (2:11–4:11). The lifestyle of Christians should be different from, yet attractive to, that of the hostile world in which
   they live (2:11–12). One facet of this lifestyle is submission
   to "every human authority" (2:13a); specifically, all believers
   should submit to the government (2:13b–17), slaves to masters
   (2:18–20), and wives to husbands (3:1–7). Christ's example
   transforms the Christian's duties (2:21–25) in order to testify
   to God's power and goodness (3:1). Christians must live in harmony with each other and, as far as possible, non-Christians
   (3:8–12). The suffering readers must respond to the hostility

they are experiencing with bold witness and attractive conduct (3:13–17). Peter uses certain OT and Jewish traditions (Gen. 6; *1 Enoch*) to exalt Christ as the victor who has declared his victory over evil powers (3:18–22). Christian lifestyles must be distinct (4:1–6) and grounded in the nearness of the end (4:7–11).

4. Christians must respond rightly to suffering (4:12–19). Elders must shepherd God's flock with the right motives, and those "who are younger" must submit to them (5:1–5a). Christians must be humble and strong in the face of opposition (5:5b–11).

5. Peter closes with final greetings (5:12–14).

B. Who Wrote 1 Peter?

The author claims to be "Peter, an apostle of Jesus Christ" (1:1), and 2 Peter appears to refer to this first letter (2 Pet. 3:1). Early testimony of Peter's authorship of this letter is strong, but many contemporary scholars deny that Peter wrote it. Their strongest argument is that the Greek of the letter is too smooth and competent for a fisherman with no formal education. But Peter may have used a well-educated scribe, and it is not impossible that he could have written it himself. Claiming that Peter wrote the letter is far less problematic than claiming that it is pseudonymous.

C. Where Was 1 Peter Written?

Peter sends greetings from "she who is in Babylon" (5:13), suggesting that this is where Peter wrote the letter. Contemporary scholars are virtually unanimous in viewing "Babylon" as a symbol for worldly power drawn from Babylon's role in relation to OT Israel. In keeping with the application of Babylon in Revelation, Peter thus refers to Rome, the center of worldly influence in his day. "She who is in Babylon" refers to the church (a grammatically feminine Greek word) in Rome.

D. When Was 1 Peter Written?

The letter almost surely was written in A.D. 62–63. A date after 63 is unlikely because it would not leave time for Peter to write his second letter before his martyrdom.

E. To Whom Was 1 Peter Written?

Peter's intended audience is mainly, if not exclusively, Gentile (1:18; 2:10; 4:3). These Christians lived in five Roman provinces of Asia Minor occupied today by the nation of Turkey (1:1). Peter's reference to "those who have preached the gospel to you" (1:12) suggests that he did not personally evangelize these Christians.

F. Why Was 1 Peter Written?

Peter comforts Christians who are being persecuted for their faith (1:6; 3:13–17; 4:12–19). Romans regarded Christians with suspicion and hostility because Christians refused to engage in the quasireligious customs surrounding the official Roman governmental structures, resolutely set themselves against some of the prevalent immoral practices, and met so often on their own to celebrate the Lord's Supper. The readers of 1 Peter were probably being criticized, mocked, discriminated against, and perhaps even brought into court on trumped-up charges. Peter exhorts them to witness to a hostile but watchful world by exhibiting "piety under pressure" as a means to glorify God.

G. What Does 1 Peter Contribute to Our Understanding of the Faith?

1. Use of the Old Testament. With the exception of Hebrews and Revelation, no other book in the New Testament depends so heavily on the OT. It quotes the OT eight times, alludes to it much more often, and is suffused with OT concepts and vocabulary.

2. Hope. Peter comforts suffering Christians by emphasizing hope, a confident expectation of their future glorification (e.g., 1:3–12).

3. People of God. Peter comforts suffering Christians by repeatedly applying OT language of Israel to Christians, reminding them of their identity as the people of God. Examples include "inheritance" (1:4), "God's household" (4:17), the new temple, a "spiritual house" (2:5), a "chosen people, a royal priesthood, a holy nation" called out to declare God's wondrous works (2:9). This language is all the more remarkable when we remember that Peter's readers are, at least mainly, Gentiles. (However, we

should be careful not to assume that Peter is indicating a "transfer" of privileges and titles from Israel to the church.)
4. Christ. Peter comforts suffering Christians by grounding their hope and identity in Christ's death, resurrection, ascension, and return.
   a. The blessings that believers now enjoy or hope to enjoy are rooted in Christ's death and resurrection (1:3, 18–21; 2:24–25; 3:18; 4:1).
   b. Jesus' victory over evil spiritual beings, proclaimed at his ascension, means that Christians need not fear their power (3:14, 19–22).
   c. Jesus' return in glory will usher in the time of salvation and blessing for the people of God (1:7, 13; 5:4).
   d. While Jesus' acts provide the basis on which Christians can experience God's grace now and in the future, they also stand as a model for Christians to imitate. As he suffered and entered into glory (1:11), so must those who belong to him (4:13; cf. 5:1). Suffering Christians should imitate their Savior, who did not revile his persecutors but entrusted himself to God (2:21–23).

H. Questions for Review and Discussion

1. Why did Peter write this letter?
2. How does this letter comfort persecuted Christians?

I. Recommended Resources

Introductory

Clowney, Edmund. *The Message of 1 Peter*. BST. Downers Grove: InterVarsity Press, 1988.

Intermediate

Grudem, Wayne A. *The First Epistle of Peter*. TNTC. Grand Rapids: Eerdmans, 1988.

Marshall, I. Howard. *1 Peter*. IVPNTC. Downers Grove: InterVarsity Press, 1991.

Schreiner, Thomas R. *1, 2 Peter, Jude*. NAC 37. Nashville: Broadman & Holman, 2003.

chapter twenty-two

2 PETER

A. What Is 2 Peter About?

1. Peter opens with a greeting that gives a theological description of the readers (1:1–2) and exhorts them based on God's gifts and promises (1:3–11). He writes as if on his deathbed, reminding them one last time of the truth they must embrace (1:12–15).
2. Christians can have absolute confidence that Jesus will come again: at Jesus' transfiguration Peter and other apostles glimpsed Jesus' future glory, and the prophets—utterly reliable because the Spirit speaks through them—confirm the same truth (1:16–21).
3. Peter denounces false teachers (2:1–22): He introduces and describes them (2:1–3a); condemns them using OT examples, thereby reassuring his readers about the ultimate fate of the false teachers (2:3b–10a); describes them as arrogant, sensual, and greedy (2:10b–16); and again describes and condemns them (2:17–22).
4. Peter encourages his readers to "remember" the teaching of the Lord and the prophets, who clearly predicted the Lord's coming and the day of judgment (3:1–13). The false teachers deny this coming intervention, deliberately forgetting that God has directly intervened before in creation and the flood.
5. Peter closes with a final exhortation and doxology (3:14–18). He frames the letter with references to grace and knowledge (1:2; 3:18a).

B. Who Wrote 2 Peter?

The letter claims to have been written by "Simon Peter, a servant and apostle of Jesus Christ" (1:1), a claim bolstered by personal reminiscence (1:13–16). For no other NT letter, however, is there a greater consensus among scholars that the person who is named as the author is not the author. We are left with the choice of accepting the letter's claim or viewing it as a forgery hardly deserving of inclusion in the Bible.

The arguments against Peter's authorship are not finally conclusive, so we conclude that Peter wrote it.

C. When and Where Was 2 Peter Written?

Peter likely wrote this letter shortly before 65, when reliable early tradition records his martyrdom during Nero's persecution of Christians in Rome. He is almost certainly writing from Rome, and he senses that the time for the fulfillment of the Lord's prophecy about his death had come (cf. 1:13–14; John 21:18–19). Identifying the false teachers he refers to would help us pin down the date and circumstances of the letter, but we do not have enough evidence, since Peter is more interested in condemning the false teaching than in describing it.

D. To Whom Was 2 Peter Written?

Peter addresses his letter to "those who through the righteousness of our God and Savior Jesus Christ have received a faith as precious as ours" (1:1). The lack of specifics led Christians in the past to classify 2 Peter as a "general" or "catholic" letter addressed generally to the church worldwide. But the letter suggests a definite audience since the readers are threatened by a specific false teaching and have apparently received, or are aware of, at least two letters of Paul (3:15). Peter appears to allude to 1 Peter by calling this "my second letter to you" (3:1), which would mean that his audience is mainly Gentiles. By using religious language with which his readers would have been familiar, Peter contextualizes the gospel to meet their needs.

E. Why Was 2 Peter Written?

Peter's purpose is to encourage his readers to mature in their understanding and practice of God's grace in Christ (3:18) because they are threatened by false teaching that might cut off their growth. For this reason, negative descriptions of and warnings about false teachers dominate the letter.

F. Do Jude and Peter Borrow from Each Other?

Jude and 2 Peter denounce false teachers with very similar language (cf. Jude 4, 6–9, 12, 18 with 2 Pet. 2:1, 3–4, 6, 10–11, 13, 17; 3:3). Since the order is similar and many words and expressions are not used elsewhere in the Bible, some kind of relationship probably exists between the two letters. The two most likely options are that Peter borrowed from Jude or that Jude borrowed from Peter, but we do not know who borrowed from whom.

G. What Does 2 Peter Contribute to Our Understanding of the Faith?

1. The seriousness of error. Theological and moral error go hand-in-hand, and both are serious matters that Peter condemns (2:4, 9, 12–13, 17, 20–21).
2. Day of the Lord. This world is destined to be "destroyed" by fire (cf. Isa. 30:30; 66:15–16; Nah. 1:6; Zeph. 1:18; 3:8) and transformed into a "new heaven and a new earth" (2 Pet. 3:7–13).
3. Memory. Christians must remember — not merely intellectually, but in practice — the teaching they have already received (1:12–15; 3:1, 5, 8).

H. Questions for Review and Discussion

1. Why did Peter write this letter?
2. Is there a relationship between wrong theology and morality? Explain.

I. Recommended Resources

Introductory

Moo, Douglas J. *2 Peter and Jude*. NIVAC. Grand Rapids: Zondervan, 1996.

Intermediate

Charles, J. Daryl. "2 Peter" and "Jude." Pages 357–411, 539–69 in *Hebrews–Revelation*. Rev. ed. EBC 13. Grand Rapids: Zondervan, 2006.

Schreiner, Thomas R. *1, 2 Peter, Jude*. NAC 37. Nashville: Broadman & Holman, 2003.

chapter twenty-three

1, 2, 3 JOHN

A. What Are 1, 2, and 3 John About?

1 John

This is a pastoral letter to a congregation or to a number of congregations. Its structure is disputed, largely because John keeps returning to the same themes from slightly different angles. He lays down three tests: True believers must believe that Jesus is the Christ come in the flesh, and this *faith* must work itself out in *righteousness* and *love*.

1. Prologue (1:1–4)
2. Fellowship with God is walking in the light (1:5–2:17).
3. John deals directly with the present situation of the church or churches to which he writes (2:18–3:24).
4. Certain tests distinguish those who belong to God from the "world" (4:1–5:12).
5. Conclusion (5:13–21)

2 John

1. Introduction (1–3)
2. The central section (4–11) warns against the dangers posed by traveling preachers, some of whom are "deceivers, who do not acknowledge Jesus Christ as coming in the flesh." But even here, John insists that true believers walk not only in the truth but in transparent love for one another.
3. Conclusion (12–13)

3 John

1. Introduction (1–4)

2. Body (5–12). John commends the church for supporting itinerant gospel-preachers and then compares two men in the church. Diotrephes not only "loves to be first" but has become so powerful that he is refusing John's representatives and ejecting from the church those who take a softer line. John encourages Gaius to follow Demetrius's example of integrity and consistently good behavior and announces that he is coming to expose Diotrephes.
3. Conclusion (13–14)

B. Who Wrote 1–3 John?

Writings from the end of the first century and the first half of the second century allude to 1–3 John, and others specifically identify the author as the apostle John. Never have these books been attributed to anyone other than John the apostle, the son of Zebedee. Furthermore, the letters themselves suggest that John is the author because their themes, words, and arrangements of words and phrases are so similar to those of John's gospel (see section G).

By designating himself "the elder" (2 John 1; 3 John 1), John may have been emphasizing his pastoral role (cf. 1 Pet. 5:1), his age (cf. Philem. 9), or both. He was *an* apostle, not *the* apostle (cf. Rom. 1:1; 1 Pet. 1:1), but he could be *the* elder in the Ephesus region, precisely because he was not just an ordinary elder. The author writes as an eyewitness with his fellow apostles (1 John 1:1, 3; 4:14; 5:6–7), with authority across congregations (2–3 John).

C. Where Were 1–3 John Written?

John most likely wrote from Ephesus. The evidence indicates that he moved to Ephesus at the time of the Jewish War (66–70) and ultimately died there.

D. When Were 1–3 John Written?

We cautiously date John's gospel at 80–85 (see ch. 6) and John's letters in the early 90s. John likely wrote the letters after his gospel because they refute proto-Gnosticism (see below), which was on the rise at the end of the first century.

E. To Whom Were 1–3 John Written?

In 1 John no addressee is mentioned, and there are no specific greetings or any formal touch such as would normally characterize a first-century letter. It was probably intended for a church or churches.

The second letter is addressed to "the lady chosen by God and . . . her children." This almost certainly refers not to an actual woman and her family but to a local church or churches.

In his third letter John addresses an individual by the name of Gaius, an exceedingly common name in the Roman Empire.

The recipients of these letters were probably located somewhere around Ephesus, perhaps including the territory spanned by the seven churches of Revelation 2–3.

F. Why Were the Letters of John Written?

John writes these letters in response to false teaching that is pervading the church (1 John 2:26–27). Some professing believers have already withdrawn (1 John 2:18–19), and John warns his readers about false teachers who are actively trying to deceive them (2:26). John calls the opponents "false prophets" (1 John 4:1), "deceivers" (2 John 7), and "antichrists" (1 John 2:18; 4:3; 2 John 7). He reassures the faithful by (a) explaining the differences between themselves and those who merely profess to be Christians, and (b) giving them grounds for their own assurance and confidence before God (1 John 5:13) at a time when they were being made to feel inferior and spiritually threatened.

The false teachers denied that the human Jesus was the Christ (1 John 2:22–23; 2 John 9; cf. 1 John 4:15) who came in the flesh (1 John 4:2; 2 John 7) and that they were in any sense subject to sin (1 John 1:6–10). This false teaching was probably based on an early form of Gnosticism, a diverse blend of Jewish, Christian, and pagan deviations that views matter as evil and spirit (what is non-material) as good. According to this heresy, people may be delivered from their (evil) flesh by acquiring knowledge (*gnosis*). Christ was not fully human because then he would possess an evil material body. This is why John stresses that Jesus is Christ come in the flesh.

Full-blown Gnosticism, however, almost certainly flowered *after* the writing of the New Testament. This movement was likely gaining strength when John wrote his letters, so John is most likely refuting an incipient, embryonic, proto-Gnosticism—perhaps one of the following:

1. Docetism: This branch of Gnosticism argues that Christ could not actually *become* flesh (evil by definition) since he is a

spirit-being (good by definition). Christ merely *appeared* to be human.

2. Cerinthianism: This branch of Gnosticism is named after the heretic Cerinthus, who distinguished between Jesus and Christ. Jesus was an ordinary human being, and Christ was a divine aeon (i.e., a spiritual power deriving from the supreme deity) who came upon Jesus at his baptism and left him to suffer alone on the cross.

These views seem to match the false teaching in John's letters, although neither matches perfectly.

The specific purpose of 2 John is primarily to warn a congregation or house church against admitting traveling teachers who espouse such false teaching. The third letter is perhaps nothing other than a warning against someone who is attempting to appropriate all local authority. Even so, because this was taking place against the background established by the other two letters, we might speculate that Diotrephes was using heresy to build his own power base.

G. How Do John's Letters Compare with John's Gospel?

Although the letters have some subtle differences, their vision and thought are complementary, not contradictory. The same stark polarities prevail: light and darkness, life and death, truth and falsehood, love and hate. For example, 1 John and John's gospel speak of salvation similarly: in our unredeemed state we are of "the devil," who has sinned and lied and murdered "from the beginning" (1 John 3:8 and John 8:44); we are from "the world" (2:16; 4:5 and 8:23; 15:19); therefore, we "sin" and are guilty of sin (3:4; 1:8 and 8:34; 9:41), "walk in the darkness" (1:6; 2:11 and 8:12; 12:35), and are "dead" (3:14 and 5:25). God loved us and sent his Son to be "the Savior of the world" (4:14 and 4:42) so that "we might live" and "have eternal life" (4:9 and 3:15,16,36). Believing in his "name" (5:13 and 1:12), we pass "from death to life" (3:14 and 5:24). We "have life" (5:12 and 20:31) from God, for life is "in his Son" (5:11–12 and 1:4). This is what it means to be "born of God" (2:29; 3:9; 4:7; 5:4, 18 and 1:13).

H. What Do John's Letters Contribute to Our Understanding of the Faith?

1. Non-negotiable doctrine. It is critically important that the church test all attempts to rearticulate the gospel. The stan-

dard is God's unchanging, non-negotiable gospel revelation. John's opponents saw themselves as the cutting edge of Christian reflection (2 John 9), but John unflinchingly guards the gospel. This stance has a bearing on what teachings a church will listen to (2 John). At the practical level, whether or not heresy stands behind 3 John, there is no place for petty gurus in the church who will not bow to apostolic admonition and authority.

2. Assurance. While other NT writings objectively ground our confidence before God in Christ and his death and resurrection on our behalf, such that Christian assurance accompanies genuine faith, John's letters distinguish between genuine and spurious faith. Those with genuine faith have assurance before God by (1) the validity of its object — Jesus is Christ come in the flesh — and (2) the transformation it effects in the individual — increased righteousness and love.

3. Late first-century church. John's letters give us a glimpse at what the NT church was like at the end of the apostolic age. He emphasizes eternal life that was with the Father and has been mediated by the Son (1 John 1:2); the Son's atonement (2:1–2; 3:8; 4:10; 5:6); and the Holy Spirit (2:20–27; 3:24–4:6). These letters enable one to compare the church of the earliest NT writings with the late first-century church, and they likewise continue the trajectory that stretches out toward the second- and third-century church.

I. Questions for Review and Discussion

1. What are the three tests in 1 John?
2. What is Gnosticism, and what does it have to do with these letters?
3. What does 1 John teach about Christian assurance?

J. Recommended Resources

Introductory

Carson, D. A. "The Johannine Letters." Pages 351–55 in *New Dictionary of Biblical Theology*. Edited by T. Desmond Alexander and Brian S. Rosner. Downers Grove: InterVarsity Press, 2000.

Intermediate

Stott, John R. W. *The Letters of John*. 2d ed. TNTC. Grand Rapids: Eerdmans, 1988.

Advanced

Kruse, Colin G. *The Letters of John*. PNTC. Grand Rapids: Eerdmans, 2000.

chapter twenty-four

JUDE

A. What Is Jude About?

Jude's letter is brief yet full.

1. Opening (vv. 1–2)
2. Jude states his reason for writing: false teachers have invaded the church (vv. 3-4). He exposes and condemns the false teachers in three stages (vv. 5–10, 11–13, 14–16) by using illustrations and quotations from the Old Testament and from Jewish writers.
3. The apostles predicted that these scoffers would arise (vv. 17–19). The readers must keep themselves in God's love (vv. 20–21) and reach out to those affected by the false teaching (vv. 22–23).
4. Jude concludes with a now-famous doxology (vv. 24–25).

B. Who Wrote Jude?

The author is "Jude, a servant of Jesus Christ and a brother of James" (v. 1). This James is almost certainly the man who became a prominent leader in the early church (see Acts 15:13–21; 21:18; Gal. 2:9) and wrote the NT letter of James. Since this James was also a "brother of the Lord" (Gal. 1:19; see also Mark 6:3/Matt. 13:55; John 7:5), the Jude of verse 1 is "Judas," the brother of Jesus mentioned in the gospels (Mark 6:3; Matt. 13:55). The witness of the early church confirms this conclusion, and arguments against it are weak.

C. When and Where Was Jude Written?

The letter cannot be dated after about 90, the latest we can realistically expect even a younger brother of Jesus to have lived. Jude and

2 Peter describe similar false teaching, suggesting that they were written at about the same time. We date 2 Peter to 64–65, so we should probably date Jude in the middle-to-late 60s. Nothing certain can be determined about where the letter was written; we don't know whether Jude stayed in Palestine all his life.

D. To Whom and Why Was Jude Written?

Although it is traditionally categorized as a "general" letter, Jude wrote to a definite church or group of churches. The readers were probably Jewish-Christian, perhaps set in the midst of a Gentile culture.

Jude writes because false teachers "have secretly slipped in among" his readers (v. 4). He condemns the false teachers for their wicked lifestyle: they are sexually immoral (vv. 4,8), scornful of authority (vv. 8–10), selfish (v. 12), and boastful (v. 16). Jude and 2 Peter probably address the same general "movement" of false teaching, with some possible difference in emphasis. Jude's description is too vague to allow precise identification.

E. What Does Jude Contribute to Our Understanding of the Faith?

1. False teaching. Although people do not like to dwell on the negative, it is important to understand that (1) false teachers exist, (2) their teaching can be both attractive and dangerous, and (3) their condemnation is certain. Jude makes these points by associating the false teachers with sinners, rebels, and heretics in the OT and Jewish tradition. We can expect defections from truth and morality in every generation. The atmosphere of postmodernism in which the church now lives requires us to guard vigilantly against the temptation to welcome heresy in the name of "tolerance."

2. Canon. In addition to several possible allusions, Jude refers to two stories not taught in the Bible: the story of Michael's dispute with the devil over Moses' body in verse 9 (apparently from *The Assumption of Moses*) and the prophesy of Enoch in verses 14–15 (from *1 Enoch* 1:9, a Jewish writing from the OT Pseudepigrapha). Some wrongly conclude from this that the standard set of Old Testament books (i.e., the OT "canon") was not fixed in Jude's day. Yet Jude cites neither of these books as "Scrip-

ture," nor does he use traditional formulas to introduce them. He implies nothing about his view of the books in which they are found. He may cite them simply because they are well known to his audience.

F. Questions for Review and Discussion

1. How would you state the theme of this letter in one sentence?
2. How might Jude's warning against false teachers apply to your context?

G. Recommended Resources

Introductory

Moo, Douglas J. *2 Peter and Jude.* NIVAC. Grand Rapids: Zondervan, 1996.

Intermediate

Charles, J. Daryl. "2 Peter" and "Jude." Pages 357 – 411, 539 – 69 in *Hebrews – Revelation.* Rev. ed. EBC 13. Grand Rapids: Zondervan, 2006.

Schreiner, Thomas R. *1, 2 Peter, Jude.* NAC 37. Nashville: Broadman & Holman, 2003.

chapter twenty-five

REVELATION

A. What Is Revelation About?

The structure of Revelation is hotly debated, mainly because it radically affects one's understanding of the book.

1. Prologue (1:1–20). John opens with an introduction (1:1–3), greeting (1:4–8), and vision of the glorified Christ (1:9–20).
2. Messages to seven churches (2:1–3:22). The risen Christ commands John to write messages to seven churches in seven cities within the Roman province of Asia: Ephesus, Smyrna, Pergamum, Thyatira, Sardis, Philadelphia, and Laodicea.
3. A vision of heaven (4:1–5:14). In heaven John sees the sovereign God seated on the throne and receiving worship. This sets the stage for the drama that unfolds: a sealed scroll is in God's hand, and only "a Lamb, looking as if it had been slain" is worthy to break the seven seals and open the scroll.
4. The seven seals (6:1–8:5). John describes what he sees as the Lamb opens six seals: conquest, slaughter, famine, death, martyrs crying out for justice, and natural disasters (6:1–17). Then John sees two visions: 144,000 people from the tribes of Israel who had been sealed by God (7:1–8) and an innumerable multitude who had "come out of the great tribulation" (7:9–17). Opening the seventh seal brings silence in heaven and introduces the seven trumpets (8:1–5).
5. The seven trumpets (8:6–11:19). John observes the disasters that come upon the earth as angels blow the first six trumpets: hail and fire from heaven (8:7), a mountain thrown into the sea (8:8–9), a great star falling from the sky (8:10–11), astronomical changes (8:12–13), destructive locusts (9:1–12), and a huge conquering

army (9:13–21). Two visions follow: an angel with a little scroll that John is instructed to eat (10:1–11) and two witnesses, who prophesy, are killed, and are raised again (11:1–14). The seventh trumpet contains no specific event but begins hymns that praise God for his triumph and judgments (11:15–19).

6. Seven significant signs (12:1–14:20). John sees seven visions: a woman gives birth to a son (12:1–6); Michael and his angels fight a dragon (Satan), who is cast out of heaven and fights the woman and her child on earth (12:7–13:1a); the world worships a beast who comes out of the sea (13:1b–10); a beast who comes out of the earth dominates the world (13:11–18); the 144,000 praise the Lamb (14:1–5); a vision of three angels (14:6–13); and a being "like a son of man" harvests the earth with the help of angels (14:14–20).

7. The seven bowls (15:1–16:21). John sees "seven angels with the seven last plagues" (15:1). Those who had triumphed over the beast sing praises to God as the angels come out of the temple with the plagues (15:2–8), which are seven bowls that the angels successively pour out on the earth (16:1): painful sores "on the people who had the mark of the beast and worshiped his image" (16:2); the sea turned into blood (16:3); the rivers and springs turned into blood (16:4–7); scorching heat from the sun (16:8–9); destruction of the beast's dominion (16:10–11); the Euphrates River dried up and the coming of evil spirits for "the battle" at Armageddon (16:12–16); and, climactically, the "It is done!" of utter earthly destruction (16:17–21).

8. The triumph of Almighty God (17:1–21:8). These visions describe and celebrate God's sovereign triumph in the world and the world to come. God judges the wicked and rewards the righteous. John sees the evil and destiny of Babylon, representing an ungodly suppressor of God's people (17:1–18). God condemns and destroys Babylon and those who profited from her mourn (18:1–19:5). A great multitude who had been invited to share in the wedding supper of the Lamb praises God (19:6–10). The rider on a white horse defeats the beasts and assembled nations (19:11–21). John describes the "thousand years" (or "millennium"): Satan is bound, and "the first resurrection" occurs (20:1–6). Satan leads the final rebellion, and God destroys him (20:7–10) and judges all the dead before the great white throne (20:11–15). The passing of the first earth leads to John's vision of "a new heaven and a new earth" (21:1), in which God resides

with his people (21:2–5) and the righteous are separated from the wicked (21:6–8).

9. The new Jerusalem (21:9–22:9). John sees the "bride, the wife of the Lamb," in the image of a new Jerusalem, whose features and dimensions are described in considerable detail (21:9–21). There will be no need for temple or sun or moon in this city, for God and the Lamb are there, and there will be no wickedness (21:22–22:5). John climaxes his prophecy by quoting Jesus' promise to come again soon (22:6–9; cf. 22:12, 20).

10. Epilogue (22:10–21). The message John saw is "trustworthy and reliable." There will be reward for those who are faithful and true, and this reward is brought by Jesus himself, who is "coming quickly."

B. Who Wrote Revelation?

Revelation claims to have been written by "John, your brother and companion in the suffering and kingdom and patient endurance that are ours in Jesus" (1:9; also 1:1,4; 22:8). He makes no other claims about himself, which suggests that he was well known to his readers. Which John would have been better known to the churches of Asia Minor in the late first century other than John the apostle? Reliable early church tradition, which places the apostle John in Ephesus at the end of his life, testifies that he wrote Revelation.

Some argue that Revelation's style is too different from John's gospel or letters for John to be the author. Yet it must be pointed out that different types of literature involve different writing styles. Furthermore, while Revelation may indeed have some stylistic differences, it also shares many stylistic similarities with John's other writings.

C. Where Was Revelation Written?

John writes from Patmos (1:9), a rocky and rugged island about six miles wide and ten miles long, located some forty miles southwest of Ephesus in the Aegean Sea. John was exiled there "because of the word of God testified to by Jesus" (1:9).

D. When Was Revelation Written?

The two most likely options for dating Revelation are either shortly after the Emperor Nero's reign (A.D. 54–68) or at the end of the Emperor Domitian's reign (A.D. 81–96). The oldest tradition holds to the latter (specifically the years 95–96); we are inclined to do so as well, because the conditions generally presumed in Revelation are more likely to have existed during Domitian's reign:

1. Emperor worship was an issue for Christians (13:4, 15–16; 14:9–11; 16:2; 19:20; 20:4), and Domitian ordered that he be addressed as "lord and god" (cf. 4:11), apparently making this confession a test of loyalty.
2. The letters to the seven churches are much more compatible with a date in the A.D. 90s than one in the 60s. For example, the city of Laodicea was destroyed by an earthquake in 60–61, yet the Laodicean church of Revelation is wealthy; a date in the 90s would give plenty of time for such recovery. Additionally, the church at Smyrna may not even have existed until 60–64.

E. To Whom and Why Was Revelation Written?

John directs the record of his visions to seven churches in the Roman province of Asia. John probably knew these churches from his years of ministry in the area, and all of them were located in cities that were centers of communication.

John's reason for selecting these seven churches, as well as the order in which they are listed, probably has to do with geography and communications. As William Ramsay pointed out long ago, the cities in which the churches are located are all centers of communication; a messenger bearing Revelation to the cities would arrive from Patmos in Ephesus, travel by secondary road north to Smyrna and Pergamum, and then go east on the Roman road to Thyatira, Sardis, Philadelphia, and Laodicea.[1]

F. What Style of Literature Is Revelation?

Revelation combines elements of apocalypse (1:1), prophecy (1:3), and letter (1:4) in a complex way that has no close parallel in other literature. Therefore, we should not neatly label it as only one style of literature.

1. Apocalypse: Revelation is not pure apocalypse because it is not pseudonymous and it grounds hope in Jesus' past sacrifice

---

[1] William Ramsay, *The Letters to the Seven Churches of Asia* (London: Hodder & Stoughton, 1904), 171–96. See also Colin J. Hemer, *The Letters to the Seven Churches of Asia* (Grand Rapids: Eerdmans, 2000), 14–15; Barry J. Beitzel, *The Moody Atlas of Bible Lands* (Chicago: Moody, 1985), 185.

rather than a future event. General characteristics of apocalypse include the following:

    a. response to persecution

    b. claims to relate heavenly mysteries revealed by an angel or some other spiritual being

    c. pseudonymous, written in the name of great figures like Adam or Moses

    d. culminates with the breaking in of God's kingdom, which is expected in the very near future

    e. extensive symbolism in historical surveys

    f. dualistic conception of history that sharply contrasts the present sinful world with the world to come ("apocalyptic eschatology")

2. Prophecy: Some contrast prophecy with "apocalyptic," arguing that (1) prophecy looks for God's salvation to be manifested through the processes of this world rather than through a breaking in of a new world and (2) prophets claim to speak directly from the Lord. Revelation contains elements of both prophecy and apocalyptic; no rigid distinction between the two is possible. They are also combined in several Old Testament books (e.g., Daniel, Isaiah, Zechariah) and in Jesus' Olivet Discourse.

3. Letter: Revelation is a circular letter to seven churches in Asia Minor (1:4–5, 9–11), yet its content and style are not similar to typical letters.

G. What Are the Major Approaches to Interpreting Revelation?

Interpretations of Revelation typically fall under four approaches:

1. Preterist: John's visions grow out of and describe events in his own day. Those events are now *past* (hence, the label "preterist"). The symbols in the visions all refer to people, countries, and events in the world of John's day, and his purpose is to exhort his readers to remain faithful to Christ as they wait for God to deliver them into his eternal kingdom.

2. Historical: Revelation sketches history from the time of Christ to our own day. This interpretation was common in the Middle Ages and with the Reformers, who identified the beast with the papacy.

3. Idealist: Revelation's symbolism helps us understand God's person and ways with the world in a general way, not to map out a specific course of events.

4. Futurist: A consistently futurist approach holds that everything in Revelation 4 – 22 will be fulfilled in the very last days of human history. A more moderate form holds that some events of chapters 4 – 22 (particularly the earlier ones) have occurred already or will occur before the very end.

We find some truth in all four of these views, but the futurist approach comes closest to doing justice to the nature and purposes of Revelation. John adapts and modifies the apocalyptic perspective, and he describes the end in the context of his first-century situation.

H. What Does Revelation Contribute to Our Understanding of the Faith?

1. Use of the Old Testament: Revelation borrows more extensively from the OT than any other New Testament book. Most of the references come not in explicit quotations but in allusions and conceptual borrowings.

2. God's sovereignty: The vision of God on his throne receiving worship helps us to see beyond our earthly circumstances to the Lord of earth and heaven, reminding us that only God is ultimately worthy of our devotion and praise.

3. Christ's preeminence: Revelation constantly portrays Jesus in terms appropriate only to God. It is significant that the opening vision of the book is not of God the Father but of Jesus Christ (1:12 – 20) and that both God the Father and Jesus Christ are called "the Alpha and the Omega" (1:8; 22:13). The sovereign God is accomplishing his purposes on earth through the Son, very God himself.

4. Christ's cross: While Revelation focuses on Christ's glory, power, and role in judgment, the cross is never out of sight. The powerful rider on the white horse is none other than the lamb that was slain. All that Christ does to wrap up human history is rooted in his sacrificial death.

5. End of history:
   a. Future events: Of all the books in the Bible, Revelation gives the most detailed description of events at the end of history. Some may be guilty of finding far more specifics than John's

symbolism allows, but we should not go to the other extreme and ignore those details that John makes relatively clear.

b. Present-day living: It is shortsighted to think merely of what will happen in the end times, for the end shapes and informs the past and the present. Knowing how history ends helps us understand how we are to fit into it now. The New Testament makes clear that even now we are in "the last days," and Revelation reminds us of the reality and severity of evil and of active demonic forces. Conflict exists not only between the church and the world, but also within the church. Believers must be faithful.

c. God's judgment: A day will come when God will pour out his wrath and account for sin. The fate of every individual will depend on whether his or her name is "written in the Lamb's book of life." God will reward those who persevere and resolutely stand against the devil and his earthly minions, even at the cost of life itself. John's visions are a source of comfort for suffering and persecuted believers in all ages.

I. Questions for Review and Discussion

1. What kind of literature is Revelation?
2. What do you think is the best approach to interpret it?
3. How does it depict Christ?
4. What are some events that will occur at the end of history?
5. Agree or disagree: The main point of teaching about the end times is ethical (i.e., how we should live now in light of the future).

J. Recommended Resources

Introductory

Keener, Craig S. *Revelation*. NIVAC. Grand Rapids: Zondervan, 2000.

Intermediate

Morris, Leon. *The Book of Revelation*. Rev. ed. TNTC. Grand Rapids: Eerdmans, 1987.

Advanced

Mounce, Robert H. *The Book of Revelation*. NICNT. Rev. ed. Grand Rapids: Eerdmans, 1998.

chapter twenty-six

CONCLUSION

The New Testament is unique. You can study it your entire life and never master it; indeed, the aim for Christians is not so much to master it as to be mastered by it. The study of the New Testament is not an end in itself; rather, the end is to know the Lord Jesus, who is its center, and to be reconciled to the God who is its final author. The more you read it, hear it preached and taught, study it, memorize it, and meditate on it, the more you should delight in Jesus, the more your heart should be bowed in adoration, the more your will should be strengthened with resolve to obey with joy your Maker and Redeemer. The literature listed in the first chapter of this book may provide some help in guiding you to your next steps of study. Meanwhile, in the famous words of the eighteenth-century biblical scholar Johann Albrecht Bengel, "Apply yourself wholly to the text; apply the text wholly to yourself."

SCRIPTURE INDEX

This index is not exhaustive and instead includes Scriptures that are (1) referenced in chapters devoted to a different book of the Bible, or are (2) quoted. The index also includes the pagination for entire chapters corresponding to books of the Bible.

GENERAL INDEX

An Introduction to the New Testament

D. A. Carson and
Douglas J. Moo

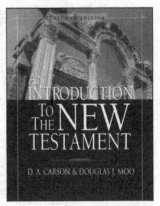

*An Introduction to the New
Testament* is the work on which
Introducing the New Testament is
based. Authors D. A. Carson and
Douglas Moo ensure that the New Testament books will be
accurately understood within historical settings by focusing
on "special introduction"—that is, historical questions dealing
with authorship, date, sources, purpose, destination, and so
forth. This approach stands in contrast to recent texts that
concentrate more on literary form, rhetorical criticism, and
historical parallels—topics the authors don't minimize, but
instead think are better given extended treatment in exegesis courses.

For each New Testament document, the authors also provide a substantial summary of that book's content, discuss the
book's theological contribution to the overall canon, and give
an account of current studies on that book, including recent
literary and social-science approaches to interpretation.

Features of the second edition include the following:

- A new chapter provides a historical survey examining
  Bible study method through the ages.
- The chapter on Paul has been expanded to include an
  analysis of debates on the "new perspective."
- The discussion of New Testament epistles has been
  expanded with a new chapter.

Hardcover, Printed: 978-0-310-23859-1

Christian Beliefs

Twenty Basics Every Christian Should Know

Wayne A. Grudem, Edited by Elliot Grudem

God doesn't call every Christian to go off to seminary, but there are certain matters of doctrine—that is, the church's teaching—that every Christian simply must know. If you are a relatively new believer in Jesus, or if you are a more mature Christian looking for a quick brush-up on basics of the faith, *Christian Beliefs* is for you.

This readable guide to twenty basic Christian beliefs is a condensation of Wayne Grudem's award-winning book on systematic theology. He and his son, Elliot, have boiled down the essentials of Christian theology and made them both clear and applicable to life. You will learn about the Bible, the characteristics of God, what it means that we are created in the image of God, what God has done for us in Christ, the purpose of the church, and much more. Each chapter includes questions for personal review or group discussion.

> Based on Systematic Theology, *this summary will certainly help beginners with Christ to get the hang of their faith.*
>
> J. I. Packer, Regent College, Vancouver, British Columbia

> *As Wayne Grudem's Systematic Theology contracts into a compact book, I do not lose my enthusiasm for the truth he loves and the clarity of his words.*
>
> John Piper, Bethlehem Baptist Church, Minneapolis, Minnesota

Softcover: 978-0-310-25599-4

The Bible and the Land

Gary M. Burge

As the early church moved away from the original cultural setting of the Bible and found its home in the West, Christians lost touch with the ancient world of the Bible. Cultural habits, the particulars of landscape, and even the biblical languages soon were unknown. The cost was enormous: Christians began to read the Bible as foreigners and miss the original images and ideas that shaped a biblical worldview.

The Bible and the Land, by New Testament scholar Gary M. Burge, launches a multi-volume series that explores how the culture of the biblical world is presupposed in story after story of the Bible. Using cultural anthropology, ancient literary sources, and a selective use of modern Middle Eastern culture, Burge reopens the ancient biblical story and urges us to look at it through new lenses. He explores primary motifs from the biblical landscape—geography, water, rock, bread, etc.—and applies them to vital stories from the Bible.

Each volume in the Ancient Context, Ancient Faith series is full-color, rich with photographs, and in a travel size for convenient Bible study anywhere you go.

Softcover: 978-0-310-28044-6

Jesus, the Middle Eastern Storyteller

Gary M. Burge

As the early church moved away from the original cultural setting of the Bible and found its home in the West, Christians lost touch with the ancient world of the Bible. Cultural habits, the particulars of land-scape, and even the biblical languages soon were unknown. The cost was enormous: Christians began to read the Bible as foreigners and miss the original images and ideas that shaped a biblical worldview.

Jesus, the Middle Eastern Storyteller, by New Testament scholar Gary M. Burge, explains that Jesus lived in a story-telling culture that was completely unlike the modern world. When we imagine Jesus' teaching in his own time and place, we cannot use profiles of teachers from our own setting to understand the nature of his work. Jesus' world was different. Burge explains the parables as they have rarely been explained before. He brings new insight to Jesus' view of God and his understanding of the life of discipleship.

Each volume in the Ancient Context, Ancient Faith series is full-color, rich with photographs, and in a travel size for con-venient Bible study anywhere you go.

Softcover: 978-0-310-28045-3

Free Online Resources at
www.zondervan.com

Zondervan AuthorTracker: Be notified whenever your favorite authors publish new books, go on tour, or post an update about what's happening in their lives at www.zondervan.com/authortracker.

Daily Bible Verses and Devotions: Enrich your life with daily Bible verses or devotions that help you start every morning focused on God. Visit www.zondervan.com/newsletters.

Free Email Publications: Sign up for newsletters on Christian living, academic resources, church ministry, fiction, children's resources, and more. Visit www.zondervan.com/newsletters.

Zondervan Bible Search: Find and compare Bible passages in a variety of translations at www.zondervanbiblesearch.com.

Other Benefits: Register yourself to receive online benefits like coupons and special offers, or to participate in research.